Diversion Books
A Division of Diversion Publishing Corp.
443 Park Avenue South, Suite 1008
New York, New York 10016
www.DiversionBooks.com

For more information, email info@diversionbooks.com

First Diversion Books edition July 2014.
Print ISBN: 978-1-62681-361-8
eBook ISBN: 978-1-62681-359-5

SACRED VOWS

The Truth About Divorce & Marriage

DANIELLE TELLER, M.D.
& ASTRO TELLER, PH.D.

DIVERSIONBOOKS

Preface

Many books have been written about how to make marriage great, and many books have also been written about how to get through divorce in one piece. This book is different. It's about society's attitudes towards marriage and divorce, and how those attitudes affect every one of us.

We were inspired to write it because of personal life events. Both of us have been divorced, and we have had the disconcerting experience of having to reevaluate our own notions about marriage and divorce. By divorcing, we also became sounding boards for friends and family trying to navigate their own marital crises. We observed firsthand the ways in which societal pressure and misinformation create unnecessary heartache for people who are already suffering through a terrible time. It seemed unfair to us that couples in the midst of a relationship crisis were made to feel shame, and that society would deliberately discourage a frank discussion about what can (or can't) reasonably be expected to improve in a failing relationship.

During our marital crises, well-meaning friends handed us self-help books with titles like *Fighting for Your Marriage*, or *Passionate Marriage*. These books take the perspective that divorce can almost always be avoided if couples follow the steps towards enlightenment set out by the authors. This perspective is fine as long as the enlightenment works for the reader. However, readers whose problems cannot be solved by these books can be left feeling like losers. These books promise one-size-fits-all solutions, but the authors of these books rarely concede that the solutions may not be a fit for every couple.

When we found ourselves in the position of counseling or consoling friends about their unhappy marriages, we wished that we had a book to give them that would say something like "Marriage is complicated. There are things that you can try to make your marriage better, but if these things don't work, don't be hard on yourself. If your spouse leaves you, or if you decide to leave your spouse, you are not a failure. Work through your problems with compassion for yourself, your spouse, and your children. Whether you stay married or get divorced, we (society) have got your back." Since that book didn't exist, we decided to write it ourselves.

Everyone has had the experience of figuring out that some long-held belief is not in fact true. For instance, you may have grown up believing that people catch colds because they don't bundle up enough in winter, and when you found out that the viruses that cause colds couldn't care less about scarves and hats, it may have seemed surprising or even a bit disorienting. This book is like that, only about marriage and divorce. Some of our cultural beliefs about marriage and divorce are quite sensible, but as you will soon realize, some don't make much sense at all.

Although we have an M.D. and a Ph.D. after our names, our areas of professional expertise are tangential to the topic of marriage and divorce. However, they are not tangential to the examination of society's attitudes towards divorce. We have been trained in fields of science that emphasize both careful critical analysis and "thinking outside the box." One of us (Astro) is a computer scientist and entrepreneur who currently oversees Google[x], Google's moonshot factory for bringing audacious scientific ideas to reality. The other of us (Danielle) is a physician specializing in the fields of intensive care and lung medicine; she has trained doctors and has run basic science research programs at the University of Pittsburgh and Harvard University. We both have had practice in questioning the status quo, and neither of us is too shy to point out the nakedness of the emperor when he happens to not be wearing clothes.

This book should be of interest to anyone who likes to question assumptions and conventional wisdom. We do not expect our readers to agree with us on every point, but we do hope to spark a new dialogue about marriage and divorce. Our goal is to hold our society's ideas up to the light of reason and ask ourselves whether we should continue to accept those ideas or not. In the words of Socrates, "True wisdom comes to each of us when we realize how little we understand about life, ourselves, and the world around us."

To be perfectly clear, we did not write this book to advocate for divorce. The desire to pair bond is one of the most basic, most compelling and most sacred of human desires. We (Astro and Danielle) are happily married, and we are passionately devoted not only to one another, but also to the concept of marriage. We wish that we lived in a world where everyone could be happily married. We don't live in that world, however. We live in a world where unsolvable relationship problems can sometimes make it impossible for people to live authentic and fulfilled lives. To be "for" marriage or "for" divorce misses the point. What this book stands "for" is the freedom to decide how to live most honestly and happily either as part of a couple or as a single person.

Although we poke fun at our society's attitudes about marriage and divorce, we never lose sight of how upsetting and frightening divorce can be. Divorce is a life-changing event that sometimes requires rebuilding an entire sense of identity. Possibly some people get divorced out of laziness, or on a whim (after all, some people go fishing with sticks of dynamite), but most people considering divorce are living in a tragic situation and responsibly trying to find a solution. The end of a marriage is sufficiently painful for individuals that the rest of society need not pile on.

If you are wondering whether you should stay married or get divorced, this book is unlikely to give you an answer. We hope, however, that this book will give you the permission to examine your feelings and your situation without shame or guilt. If you know someone else who is trying to decide whether to stay married or divorce, this book will help you to be a better friend. Finally, to everyone out there who is struggling through a marital crisis right now, we want to say, "Have hope!" Life does get better. Whether your marriage improves so that you can remain happily married, or whether your marriage ends, this crisis will pass. Work through your problems with compassion for yourself, your spouse, and your children. We've got your back.

Introduction

I'm not that sort of person

We don't mean to brag, but we think that we have some skill at mind reading. You don't believe us? Here, we will show you. We bet that we can guess your answer to the following question: "Are you the sort of person who gets divorced?"

You answered "no," didn't you? In our experience, even people who are divorced or in the process of divorcing will say, "But I'm not the sort of person who gets divorced!" In the same way that most people believe themselves to be better than average drivers (a statistical impossibility), most people also believe that they are better than the average person who divorces.

Why are we so loath to associate ourselves with the "sort of person" who divorces? Who are all of these people setting the standard for the "divorcing type"? Usually what we are trying to communicate by claiming not to be the divorcing type is "I am a loyal, responsible, morally upstanding, caring person who keeps promises." Which, of course, implies that those who divorce do not possess these qualities. We believe, perhaps subconsciously, that divorced people are not as good as people who stay married. Even those of us who are divorced like to believe that we are somehow an exception to the rule, that we are a little bit better than all those other divorced people.

When you stop to think about it, the idea that there is a monolithic "divorcing type" doesn't make a lot of sense. First, a large proportion of individuals are never even given the choice to stay married. As the old adage goes, it takes two people to stay married but only one to get divorced. Second, there are probably as many reasons for divorce as there are divorced individuals. High-rolling investment bankers have been known to divorce to reduce tax payments. King Henry VIII got divorced because his wife didn't bear him a son. Basketball player Dennis Rodman split from Carmen Electra purportedly because he was of "unsound mind" at the wedding. When you discover that someone is divorced, all you can really conclude is that he/she or his/her spouse believed that divorce was the better alternative to staying married.

The fact that many of us subconsciously believe that we are better than other people who get divorced is an example of a false cultural assumption, or what we are calling a Sacred Cow. Not every cultural belief about divorce is wrong, of course. For instance, it is conventional wisdom that divorce leads to financial hardship, and while this is not universally true, the fact that divorce is expensive can be easily substantiated. It costs more to run two households than to run one, and lawyers charge a lot of money. Thus, if someone advises you to stay married in order to save money, that person is not promoting a Sacred Cow.

Arguments against divorce that do not take the form of sweeping generalizations are not Sacred Cows either. If somebody tells you that your marriage can improve if you stick with it, we would not consider that a Sacred Cow. All marriages have ups and downs. It is often hard to know whether marital unhappiness represents a dip on the way to greater joy or the death knell of the marriage. Some unhappy marriages get better, some get worse, and some just bump along the bottom for years on end. Sorting out where your marriage is headed and what you can do to influence its course is a critical challenge, and while it's not terribly helpful to be told, "Your marriage might get better," that statement does not represent a Sacred Cow.

What then are these Sacred Cows of which we speak? Thank you for asking!

As you are undoubtedly aware, a sacred cow (lowercase) is

an idea that society does not allow to be questioned or criticized. The sacred cow is considered to be important for social stability, and challenges to the sacred cow threaten society's sense of security and cohesion. Often the sacred cow is so well established in people's minds that nobody even thinks to question its validity. For example, the "fact" that the sun went around the earth (instead of the other way around) was a sacred cow for a long, long time despite plenty of evidence to the contrary. Most people didn't question this particular sacred cow any more than you would question the structure of the solar system you learned about in school. Anyone impertinent enough to raise doubt was discouraged with ridicule, ostracism, or threats of torture and imprisonment. Now really, if an idea is a good one, it should be able to stand up for itself, right? If you tell me that your idea is true, but I'm not allowed to question it, I wonder how much confidence you have in the truth of your idea.

Similarly, the Sacred Cows of Marriage and Divorce (uppercase) are ideas designed to keep unhappy couples from choosing divorce. Just as with other sacred cows, these ideas are so deeply ingrained that most of us are only vaguely aware of the ways in which they affect our thinking. In this book, we hope to help you to recognize these Sacred Cows in your conversations and encourage you to give them a good push to see if they tip over. Ideas that are true will stand grazing unperturbed, whereas ideas with little substance will topple quite easily. We invite you,

Has anyone ever tipped over a real cow? Probably not. Cows don't actually sleep standing up, and they weigh over half a ton. Margo Lillie, a doctor of zoology at the University of British Columbia, estimated that tipping a cow would require 2,910 newtons of force even if one assumed the cow to be a rigid, inanimate object that does not respond to its surroundings. Four people working together might be able to tip a life-sized statue of a cow, but it is extremely unlikely that they could ever tip a real cow. Fortunately, our Sacred Cows are pushovers compared with real cows!

the reader, to be the judge of what is true and what is a Sacred Cow. So put on your galoshes, and let's head into the pasture to see if we can spot some of these irksome bovines.

Getting to know the Sacred Cows of Marriage and Divorce

Most of us in the Western world do not think of actual cows as holy, and so it may seem quaint or a little eccentric to us that cows are allowed to wander free and wreak havoc in some cities in India. The treatment of cows in India is complex, however. India is a nation made up of multiple religions, and even people belonging to the same religion do not necessarily agree about whether or how cows are to be revered. For some, the sacredness of cows is a deadly serious issue. Gandhi said, "The central fact of Hinduism is cow protection." For others, cows are just a convenient and delicious source of dinner.

The attitudes surrounding marriage and divorce in America today are not so different from attitudes about cows in modern India. A significant number of Americans believe divorce to be a violation of religious dictates. Many other Americans do not oppose divorce on religious grounds but still feel queasy about its morality. Still others take an entirely utilitarian view and pass no moral judgment whatsoever, only weighing the potential good and bad of each separate case. These various attitudes can prevent individuals in our society from communicating clearly with one another about marriage and divorce. Moreover, the combination of these attitudes in any one person's mind can give rise to contradictory and sometimes irrational convictions.

People who believe that marriage contracts should never be broken deserve as much respect as the people who disagree with them. Our goal is not to try to change anybody's mind about whether divorce is moral or ethical. Religious beliefs about divorce are not what we are calling "Sacred Cows." In fact, anyone who believes that marriage vows are inviolable can come right out and say, "Divorce is wrong!" as a matter of

faith, without needing to hide behind a bunch of .
As you will soon understand, the Sacred Cows rear
when people are not being sincere about their obje
divorce, or when they employ a double standard on the .   ..
The lack of sincerity may not be intentional; often, peopie are
simply not clear with themselves about what they think and feel.
Whether intentional or not, however, bringing Sacred Cows to
the conversation always adds confusion.

The Sacred Cows we address in this book are false cultural
assumptions that raise the emotional cost of divorce or cause
unnecessary fear and shame about the consequences of divorce.
These Sacred Cows have infiltrated our societal subconscious,
and many of us are unaware of the influence these assumptions
have over our thoughts and words. If you have ever counseled
an unhappy friend to stay married, however, you have probably
trotted out a few of these Cows yourself. Here is a list of the
Cows and the beliefs they represent:

The Holy Cow: Marriage is always good and divorce is
always bad (absent faith-based arguments).

The Expert Cow: All marital problems can be fixed
with the right self-help book or marriage counselor.

The Selfish Cow: Everyone who gets divorced is
selfish, and everyone who stays married is selfless.

The Defective Cow: If you cannot make your marriage
happy, or if you choose to divorce, you must be
defective in some way.

The Innocent Victim Cow: Children's lives are ruined
by divorce.

The One True Cow: Finding true love should be your
highest goal in life unless you are married, in which
case you should stop believing in true love.

The Other Cow: Nobody should be allowed to leave a
marriage in order to be with a new partner.

You have probably noticed that all of the above statements
are oversimplified generalizations. That is the nature of a
Sacred Cow. Sacred Cows don't make allowances for individual

circumstances, nuances or relativism. These Cows are absolutely convinced that they know best, and they think the whole world looks like a lovely Holstein dairy cow: black and white. Any time you introduce a word like "sometimes" or "uncertain" into your statements about marriage and divorce, the Sacred Cows become irritated and skulk away. We hope that this book will introduce plenty of uncertainty in your mind when it comes to pronouncements by our society, because that uncertainty will protect you and the people you care about from getting trampled by Sacred Cows.

Why we need to get clearer about Sacred Cows

Why is it important to push back against these bossy Cows? It is because they add unnecessary pain to a situation that is already plenty painful. On the famous Holmes and Rahe Stress Scale,[1] where patients were asked to rank a series of 43 life events according to level of stress, divorce ranked number 2, ahead of imprisonment or death of a close family member. Tearing apart the social fabric of your life and upsetting the people around you is extremely distressing, and Sacred Cows make it worse for everyone. To illustrate this, we have created the following thought experiment:

> Sunita has reached the conclusion that she can no longer remain married to Paul. It doesn't matter for the purposes of this example why she has reached this conclusion, but Paul and his family are hurt and furious, and Sunita feels *terrible*. Over their lifetimes, Sunita, Paul and everyone around them have subconsciously absorbed the messages of the Sacred Cows, and so they all tacitly agree that Sunita is selfish, that her children's lives will be ruined, that she is defective, and that she is a fool to expect life to improve for her if she divorces.

None of this changes Sunita's conclusion that she cannot stay married to Paul, but she feels ashamed and guilty. Because of her shame, Sunita tries to hide the fact that her marriage is crumbling instead of reaching out for support. Paul lashes out at her in his anger, and she accepts the abuse because she thinks that she deserves to be treated badly. Paul's family feels justified in calling her names and encourages Paul to demand as many concessions as possible from Sunita, because she is the guilty party destroying the marriage, whereas Paul is the innocent victim who deserves to be compensated.

After the two divorce, Sunita slowly sheds her guilt and decides that she is not a bad person. Gradually, Sunita's guilt is replaced with anger, and eventually Paul and Sunita have nothing remaining between them but bitterness and ill will.

Now imagine the same scenario without the Sacred Cows. Imagine that Sunita feels terrible, but she does not believe that she is a bad person for wanting to be out of her marriage. Imagine that Paul feels angry, but he does not feel justified in treating Sunita badly. Imagine that Sunita is not too ashamed to tell her friends, family and colleagues about what is happening, and she receives their support. Imagine that Paul's family is upset and disappointed but does not see Sunita as the guilty party and does not incite Paul to feel like a victim. In this scenario, where is the downside? Paul and Sunita both behave like grown-ups, and their self-esteem remains intact. Family and friends on both sides of their previous marriage have less ill will all the way around. It feels like a trick, doesn't it? There must be a downside somewhere, or society would not have created the Sacred Cows in the first place.

Many people will say that the downside of putting the Sacred Cows out to pasture is a less stable society. The worry is that allowing people like Sunita to divorce without condemnation and self-hatred will lead to annihilation of the nuclear family.

This, in turn, will cause our entire culture to come crumbling down, since the nuclear family is the cornerstone of our society.

Another view is that the Sacred Cows are necessary to keep people like Sunita married long enough for her to realize that she is actually happy in her marriage. Marriages have ups and downs, the argument goes, and Sunita would be a fool to divorce during one of the downswings instead of waiting for the next upswing. She will thank the Sacred Cows in a few years for applying sufficient pressure to keep her married.

These theories are not testable, and so we can't say that they are wrong. Maybe the message "You are a bad person if you divorce" is all that keeps us from devolving into savagery, and maybe everybody would be happier if they just got married and stayed married. Rightly or wrongly, however, our society also espouses the belief that individuals should be able pursue their own

Sacred Cow Flow Chart

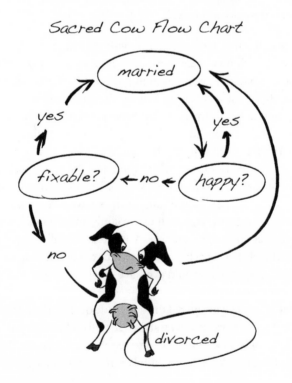

happiness and determine the course of their own lives.

Some of us may be certain that Sunita will be happiest if she stays married to Paul, and we also may believe that this country will be made stronger by the continuance of their marriage, but it is ultimately Sunita's decision whether to stay married or not. Sunita may not be perfectly able to predict what will make her happiest, but she has a better shot at figuring it out than we do. Moreover, our society has already decided that personal happiness trumps social good when it comes to marriage and divorce. One piece of evidence for this is that no-fault divorce is now legal in all 50 states in America.

We told you already that divorce ranks as the second most stressful life event. It turns out that the only event that outranks divorce is death of a spouse. In both cases a marriage is ended, but widowhood does not invite the same social censure as divorce. Perhaps the end of a marriage is cataclysmic no matter how it happens, and nobody needs the added disincentives to divorce provided by sanctimonious, meddling Sacred Cows.

The dictionary of divorce talk

When family and friends give advice to someone considering divorce, they are usually trying to be helpful. They don't always say what they really mean, however, and this can lead to confusion. This happens in other aspects of life as well, such as when you say, "Gee, Aunt Marge, I really like the sweater you knitted for me!" Sometimes you mean, "Awesome sweater!" and sometimes you mean, "I'm pleased and grateful that you love me enough to put all of that work into knitting for me, but that is one god-awful ugly sweater, and I never wear turtlenecks anyway." If Aunt Marge were aware of the alternate meaning, she wouldn't waste her time knitting you a new sweater the following Christmas, and you could be spared the guilt of putting the fruits of her labor into the Goodwill pile.

Similarly, when people offer advice or commentary about divorce, they may mean exactly what they say, but they may also be motivated by feelings or preconceived ideas that they are not even aware they possess. Nobody is trying to be two-faced, but when people comment without first examining their own motivations, they open the gate to Sacred Cows. We can't help you to decide what to take at face value and what to think a bit harder about, but we can at least offer some alternative interpretations that you may want to consider. Here is our "dictionary of divorce talk":

"Your expectations are too high. Everyone is disappointed with marriage."

Apparent meaning: You have unrealistic expectations about marriage that won't be fulfilled by your current marriage or by any potential future marriage.

Alternate interpretation: My own marriage has been disappointing to me. If you leave your spouse and find greater happiness than I have had in my life, then I will have to concede that my view that all marriages are like mine is a mistake. I may also have to conclude that I have been wasting my life in my own marriage. Therefore, I would prefer that you come to the same conclusion as I did and stay with your spouse.

"You are confused, lost."

Apparent meaning: You are behaving like a complete loon.

Alternate interpretation: I am confused. I thought that marriage, at least in our social group, was forever. You are behaving in a way that doesn't fit my paradigm of how my friends and I live our lives.

"You made a commitment and you need to stand by that commitment. Happiness is not the reason to stay married; it is staying committed that causes marital happiness."

Apparent meaning: Honoring the marriage contract will ultimately lead to happiness.

Alternate interpretation: Your marriage increases the feeling of structure and security I have in my life. If the society I live in is not stabilized by lasting marriages, then I will feel sad, insecure and worried about what other bad changes may happen around me.

"Your relationship may have problems, but it is better than being alone. You won't find someone else who will make you any happier."

Apparent meaning: I am worried that you will be lonely if you leave your marriage.

Alternate interpretation: I would never leave my marriage because I can't imagine anything worse than being single again, and I can't imagine you could feel any differently.

"But you seem like the perfect couple!"

Apparent meaning: It would be a tragedy to destroy this happy marriage.

Alternate interpretation: I value the time that we spend with your family; I like you both and enjoy being part of your circle. If you get divorced and move away, my life will be significantly impoverished. Also, if you are not happy, then who is? This makes me feel worried.

"You don't realize how lucky you are. Many people wish they could have a husband/wife as great as yours!"

Apparent meaning: Wow, your spouse is amazing and you are so lucky.

Alternate interpretation: If you're leaving your spouse because you think that you can find greater happiness elsewhere, then what does that say about me for staying with someone I judge to be a much less perfect mate than yours?

"If you're not happy in your marriage, it is because you're not working hard enough."

Apparent meaning: It really doesn't seem like you have given this marriage your best efforts yet.

Alternate interpretation: My partner isn't happy in our
    marriage and this is the lecture I give him/her all the
    time. If I'm giving my spouse this lecture, then it must
    make sense to give you the same lecture.

As this dictionary of divorce talk illustrates, people giving advice
are not always completely clear about their own motivations.
Divorces feel destabilizing to social networks; friends, family,
neighbors and colleagues may have an interest in discouraging a
couple from separating that goes beyond the personal happiness
of the divorcing spouses. They may fear losing contact with one
or both divorcé(e)s, or they may feel embarrassed that a family
member is divorcing. They may want to have their own beliefs

"How to Use This Book"

Sadly, neither Sacred Cow recognition nor Sacred Cow
tipping is likely to solve any marital problems you might
have. This book will not offer a foolproof scientifically
proven method for making your relationship wonderfully
successful and satisfying. Nor will this book help you to
make up your mind about whether to continue or to end
a troubled relationship. Only you can decide whether
the problems in your marriage can be fixed. While you
are figuring that out, however, we hope that you will
use this book to clear away unhelpful external pressure
you may be receiving from friends, family and society
at large. We also hope that this book will convince you
not to apply such pressure to friends and family in their
own marital crises. If you get to the end of this book
and decide that these aims have not been accomplished,
you could use this book as a doorstop. If you are not in
need of a doorstop, or if you are reading an electronic
version, you might consider passing the book along
to someone who has been affected by divorce or to
someone who simply enjoys deconstructing our society's
attitudes and prejudices.

and choices validated by seeing those around them make similar choices. Whatever the reason for counseling against divorce, if the reason is unrelated to the happiness of the individual contemplating divorce, then Sacred Cows will be invited to join the conversation. It does not matter whether the person giving advice is well intentioned and/or unaware of his or her motivations; Sacred Cows are pushy and will take any opening to sch*mooooz*e.

By demonstrating how Sacred Cows can muscle their way into conversations, this book will empower you to think about marriage and divorce in a new way. Although many of us do not realize it, our attitudes about marriage and divorce are tied up in cultural assumptions. The mere act of questioning those assumptions can free us from a tangle of subliminal messages we have been absorbing since childhood, allowing us to develop fresh and sometimes startling perspectives on a subject we thought we knew so well.

Now if you are ready to do some Sacred Cow tipping, read on …

References
1. Holmes T.H., Rahe R.H. (1967). The Social Readjustment Rating Scale. *Journal of Psychosomatic Research*, 11(2), 213–218.

CHAPTER ONE
The Holy Cow

*For some reason, we see divorce as a signal of failure, despite
the fact that each of us has a right, and an obligation, to rectify
any other mistake we make in life.*
—Joyce Brothers

Meet the Cow

The Holy Cow is the most self-righteous of the Sacred Cows. She believes that divorce is a personal failure and that married people are better than divorced people. Her mission is to sell everyone on the idea that the commitment of marriage should trump personal happiness, and she uses spurious data and anecdotes to shore up her argument. She believes that marriage is critical to a stable society and works to keep marriages intact for the sake of society rather than for the sake of individuals.

Caveat: Tipping over the Holy Cow does not mean that commitments are unimportant to individuals or to society. It only means that commitments should not be unalterable over the course of a lifetime.

Divorce = Failure

When asked why all of her marriages had failed, anthropologist Margaret Mead is said to have replied, "I beg your pardon; I have had three marriages and *none* of them was a failure." This statement (apocryphal or not) highlights our social tendency to equate divorce with failure. Culturally, we believe that divorce reflects weakness and selfishness, and the "failure" label applies not only to marriages, but also to the people who divorce. Our society does not like quitters, and divorce is seen as a form of quitting.

While divorce is unquestionably more socially acceptable today than it was sixty years ago, the stigma of divorce may currently be increasing, at least among educated and upper-middle-class Americans. Laurie Essig, a professor of sociology at Middlebury College, says that among the relatively affluent, "divorce has become a source of shame, a mark of failure, a sign that you just aren't working hard enough."

According to the National Marriage Project at the University of Virginia, the 10-year divorce rate for college-educated Americans has fallen to 11%, compared to a rate of almost 37% for the rest of the population. Individuals in this demographic may have few or no friends who are divorced, leading to an attitude that "our kind don't divorce." Those who choose to divorce (or have divorce thrust upon them) may be considered a threat by their married friends or may be stigmatized by former friends who believe that divorce is an act of weakness and selfishness.

The Holy Cow is an energetic promoter of this stigma. She believes that breaking marriage vows makes someone de facto a bad person. Of course, anyone divorcing *could* be a bad person; some bad people certainly do get divorced. When we reviewed the marital history of some of the most evil people on record, we found a mixed bag of histories. Joseph Stalin was widowed twice, though rumor has it that he drove his second wife to suicide. Adolf Hitler was married for only 40 hours before he and his wife committed suicide together. Idi Amin was a polygamist who married at least six women, three of whom he divorced, and one of whom was found dismembered (though by whom we do not know). Attila the Hun drowned in his own blood on his wedding night. So at least for people generally considered to be "bad," there is little pattern to their choices surrounding marriage and divorce.

Although there does not appear to be a strong correlation between a person's moral character and marital status, this doesn't completely answer the Holy Cow's accusation. In her view, marriage is always good and divorce is always bad. That means that you can prove that you are a good person by agreeing to a marriage contract, but you *become* a bad person if you break

When the libertarian social scientist Charles Murray was interviewed on NPR about his book *Coming Apart: The State of White America, 1960-2010*, he argued that the educated class of white America has something to teach the poorer, less well-educated class. In his words, upper-middle-class Americans "are getting married and staying married. They work like crazy. They do better going to church. [They should] just say that 'These are not choices we've made for ourselves. … These are rich, rewarding ways of living.'" One could quibble with all of these value judgments, because going to church or working like crazy might not be rich or rewarding for everyone. What interested us, however, was the tacit agreement between the speaker and the interviewer that "getting married and staying married" is a path to a better life. Really? Many of us know people who have vacationed in Hawaii and have been made happy by the experience. That doesn't mean that everyone in Hawaii is happy or living rich, fulfilling lives, however. Insisting that people go to Hawaii and never leave again is unlikely to cure social ills, and it certainly won't make most people substantially happier. Likewise, pushing people to marry and stay married is unlikely to increase personal happiness or social good.

that contract. To explore this Cow's attitude further, let us begin by examining the nature of the contract itself.

The marriage contract

The term "marriage contract" is so familiar that nobody bothers to define it, but have you ever asked yourself what exactly is being promised at a modern wedding? Most marriage vows contain some version of "I promise to love you forever," which is generally considered to be the core of the wedding contract. Some marriage vows are more conservative and only promise undying faithfulness, not undying love. This typically takes a form such as "for better, for worse, for richer, for poorer, in sickness and in health, until death do us part." The love is usually implied, however. Wedding guests imagine the couple in later years celebrating anniversaries with grandchildren or emotionally supporting one another through periods of unemployment, not saying, "My spouse is an ass, but I promised until death do us part, so I guess I'm stuck."

Assuming that the contract either states or implies undying love, what does it mean to promise that your feelings for someone else will never change? If you were applying for your dream job, you would never sign a contract that said, "I not only promise never to leave this job, but I promise to be equally enthusiastic about working here for the rest of my life, no matter how this job evolves and no matter how much I change as a person." Yet this is more or less what most of us do when we get married. We promise that we are going to continue to feel the way we do today in perpetuity, even though experience teaches us that our feelings about most things change over time. Anyone who has gone grocery shopping after eating a large meal knows how context affects our prediction of our own future feelings. The return of hunger seems inconceivable, and somehow yogurt and celery seem like more than enough groceries for the week.

Similarly, people who are rapturous on their wedding day cannot conceive of ever feeling differently. As we all know, however, the inconceivable does sometimes end up happening: couples do fall out of love. It turns out that people are not all that good at predicting how they will feel in a decade, and neither can they make themselves feel an emotion in perpetuity simply by promising to do so.

If we took a more clear-eyed view of the marriage contract, what might it look like? Assuming that it is not truly within our power to promise to feel a certain way 20 years hence, what could we more reasonably sign up for? Let's try out a few contracts to see which one you would consider a reasonable commitment to make:

> "I, _____, do promise to do my utmost to love you, _____, for as long as we are married. I promise that if a time comes when I do not love you, I will do everything in my power to try to rekindle that love. If I become convinced that I cannot regain my love for you, I will tell you promptly and end our marriage as elegantly as I can."

> "I, _____, do promise to act as though I love you, _____, for as long as I shall live. I promise not to leave you under any circumstance, no matter how miserable it makes me to stay with you."

> "I, _____, do promise to love you, _____, forever (even though that is not something I can really promise, as none of us has better than partial control over who we love and how we feel). I am leaving unspoken what happens if I can't continue to love you, because that is a highly uncomfortable subject right now, and I hope it never comes up. I understand that having avoided this topic now, we are in some danger of later disagreeing about exactly what I have committed to you and exactly what I need to do in order to remain in compliance with this contract."

In some ways, weddings are an exercise in group denial, or at least group optimism. Most people essentially ignore the fact that the promise of eternal love doesn't hold up to scrutiny. Nobody wants to have to say or hear anything unromantic at weddings, so the bride(s), the groom(s) and their guests just keep fingers crossed, hoping that the love will last a lifetime. Therapist and author Ester Perel summarizes it this way: "The contract shatters the romantic ideal. We are trapped by the fact that we marry for love. The thought that at the beginning of a love story you would already write what would happen if the love story ends is unfathomable to people."

The Holy Cow exploits the ambiguity created by the vague nature of the marriage contract. Few people would agree to a contract that said, "I promise to stay with you until I die no matter how badly you treat me, no matter how much I come to dislike you, no matter how unhappy it makes me to be with you." Yet the Holy Cow will point out that you did in fact promise "until death do us part," and she is not interested in having a discussion about whether or not that was a reasonable promise for you to make. The Holy Cow believes that marriage is more than just a contract between two individuals that can be dissolved by the contracting parties. The Holy Cow believes that without marriage, there would be no foundation for the family, which would cause destabilization of society and ultimately the destruction of civilization itself.

> When two people are under the influence of the most violent, most insane, most delusive, and most transient of passions, they are required to swear that they will remain in that excited, abnormal, and exhausting condition continuously until death do them part.
>
> —G.B. Shaw, *Getting Married*, 1908

The glue that binds us

Doubtless there are couples who stay in love for a lifetime, and there are also couples for whom loyalty and security are enough to sustain happiness, even if love doesn't last. Some couples grow apart, however, and become unhappy. Individuals in this circumstance are told by the Holy Cow that they should stay married, because this Cow believes that commitment trumps happiness. The Holy Cow has only one definition of a successful marriage, which is that one spouse gets to bury the other. She doesn't really care what happens along the way (though she would probably object that murder would be cheating) as long as the couple gets to the ultimate finish line, death.

The Holy Cow is not all doom and gloom, however; that would not be an effective way of getting her message across. She also promotes the positive aspects of commitment, such as the idea that marriage commitment helps people to ride out rough relationship patches, avoiding premature termination of what could otherwise have been a happy and fulfilling marriage.

It is not uncommon to hear married people say something like: "One of the most comforting parts of marriage for me is that it is binding. I know that we will weather tough times and disagreements because we are married." Undoubtedly, people who say this mean it quite sincerely. Yet when you think about it, it's an odd thing to say.

Imagine the following situation: Amir and Jennifer have been married for ten years, and they have a mostly happy life. There are several subjects about which the two of them simply cannot agree, however, and fights erupt over issues like whether Amir is pulling his weight when it comes to keeping the house clean. Their crankiness with one another can last all day (sometimes several days) until one of them initiates an apology, at which point they make heartfelt promises to do better and talk about how much they love each other. Because they truly do love one another.

Now imagine that one day while they are both still in the foulest of moods, Jennifer happens to be cleaning out the filing cabinet. She finds their marriage license and notices that the names printed on the license belong to another couple! They signed the wrong piece of paper, and they are in fact not legally married.

Remember that Jennifer just had a big fight with Amir. What does she do now that she realizes that he is not legally her husband? Does she rush to pack her bags, saying, "Thank the Lord, I can finally run away!!" Or does she bring the paper to Amir, saying, "Guess what, honey, we have been living in sin and now you need to make me an honest woman. And, since I know that you're really sorry for not doing your share of the chores, this might be the moment to buy me that diamond ring I've been eyeing …"

We are betting the latter. Amir and Jennifer love one another, and they don't want to end their relationship. The comfort that they take from being married is not the existence of the contract, but the fact that ten years ago, they said to one another, "I choose you." Jennifer knows that Amir loves her more than anyone in the whole world, and she knows that she loves him that much too.

Couples who live together without marrying can be just as committed to one another as Jennifer and Amir, but often that's not the case (at least in societies where permanent cohabitation is less the norm than marriage). Often these couples avoid marriage because one or both partners is not completely sure that the other partner is Mr. or Ms. Right. It is uncomfortable to know that you are Mr. or Ms. Good Enough for Right Now, and that your relationship could end if someone better came along. One of the reasons marriage is comforting is because married people have told one another that they are each other's favorite person in the universe.

In this way, marriage is less the cause of wanting to stay together and more the effect. Jennifer and Amir got married because they both knew that they wanted to build a life together. Finding out that they are not, in fact, married does not diminish their desire to be together, nor does it diminish their confidence that they are each other's favorite person. On the flip side, finding out that they are not actually married would not make it much easier to split up if they stopped being each other's favorite person.

To illustrate this, let's look at what happens if Jennifer doesn't love Amir anymore. She does not enjoy being around him, and they become emotionally estranged. During one of their fights, Jennifer finds the false marriage certificate. Does this make it easier to leave? Jennifer is still going to feel terrible for leaving Amir, and it will be no easier to negotiate the division of assets or custody of children if they are not legally married. The impact on their social circle and families will be identical, and if they cannot agree on terms of separation, the battle will be equally if not more difficult than a "real" divorce. We would guess that the probability of Jennifer leaving would be quite similar whether she discovered the false marriage certificate or not.

A lawyer's musings about the marriage contract

Wedding vows have all the elements of a verbal contract: a set of promises offered and accepted, the consideration being the performance of those promises by the other party. Interestingly, however, our legal system recognizes that these promises are not very realistic and does not uphold them strictly. A judge would never enforce specific performance for breach of the contract ("Edna, you promised to love him forever. Forever is not over yet. Get back in there and loooove him!"). Instead, the law seems to impose reasonable terms on marriage agreements, mainly concerned with reliance issues associated with breach of the contract. When people commit to each other through marriage, they make themselves vulnerable by relying on the other person, often to their detriment if the commitment is breached. The examples are pretty obvious: being forsaken after doing all the work to raise children, foregoing career advancement so your spouse can benefit, foregoing potentially better mates who become harder to find with advancing age, etc. Remedies provided by law do not involve specific performance, but rather monetary damages. This seems to be a practical approach that tries to help offset the negative effects of this reliance.

In the circumstance where Jennifer no longer loves him, Amir probably doesn't find the marriage contract comforting either. If he interprets the contract to mean "I will stay with you always," even if the contract were completely binding, it probably would not make Amir happy to force Jennifer to stay with him. Since the contract is not in fact binding and can be broken unilaterally, it would be no comfort even if he did want to keep Jennifer trapped and miserable. If, on the other hand, Amir interprets the contract to mean "I will love you forever," then the contract has already been broken. By no longer loving Amir, Jennifer has made the agreement meaningless.

If we were honest with ourselves, we would realize that saying, "I don't care whether some time in the future you discover that you don't love me; you are never allowed to leave me" is not a nice thing to say. We would also realize that saying, "I promised, so I'm going to darn well force myself to love you or pretend to love you until one of us dies," is not terribly realistic. Tipping the Holy Cow requires the rigor to sort out what is realistic from what is merely wishful thinking.

Triumph of hope over experience

Oscar Wilde famously said, "Marriage is the triumph of imagination over intelligence. Second marriage is the triumph of hope over experience." We have already addressed the ways in which we brush aside our understanding of human nature at weddings, but what about the second (and more famous) half of the quotation? Surely anyone who has been divorced will necessarily be cynical about "until death do us part" the second time around.

To think about this some more, let's look at a divorced couple, Greg and Rebecca. It has been five years since they split up, and Greg is engaged to a wonderful woman he has known since high school. When he tells his friend Peter about the engagement, Peter says, "Congratulations, my friend, but I don't know how you can go through this again. What makes you think that she won't dump you just like Rebecca dumped you?"

Greg, who is a logical sort of guy, replies, "I don't. I didn't know that Rebecca was going to leave me, and I don't know whether the same thing will happen with Anika, or whether I will fall out of love with her. All I can say is that I'm crazy about her right now, and I feel certain that we can have a great life together. The fact that Rebecca left me makes it no more or less likely that Anika will do the same, and so I don't see why my optimism should be less (or more) the second time around. I was happy being married, and I am really looking forward to being married again."

Wedding vows the second time around represent the triumph of hope over experience in some ways like driving a car after surviving an accident is the triumph of hope over experience. If you are a terrible driver and the accident reflects your incompetence, then you would probably be better off taking the train. However, that was equally true before your accident: you were just as foolish to drive recklessly before you crashed as you would be to drive recklessly after you crashed (although if the accident caused you to drive more carefully, just as a divorce sometimes causes spouses to behave better the second time around, the risk of crashing may actually decrease after the accident). On the other hand, if you are a pretty good driver who had bad luck, you would be irrational to reject the risk of driving after the accident when you had accepted the risk before. Assuming that you keep driving with the same caution, your risk of another smashup in the next ten years is exactly the same in two parallel universes: one where you already had an accident and one where you did not. In this way, Greg is no more or less unrealistic to promise "till death do us part" the second time around than the first.

Meanwhile, Rebecca is also planning to get remarried. While shopping for a wedding dress, Rebecca's mother expresses her concern about a second marriage, saying, "Honey, are you sure that you want to do this? The first marriage didn't go so well, so I don't see why you think that this one will be any different. Isn't the definition of insanity repeating the same mistake and expecting different results?"

Rebecca, exasperated, answers, "Mom! Just because I got divorced doesn't mean that I'm a failure at marriage. I chose to marry the wrong person. That is my cross to bear, but don't condescend to me by telling me that I can't tell when I've found the right person to marry. Making a mistake and choosing the wrong partner is not the same thing as being lousy at marriage!"

Rebecca is in a somewhat different position from Greg, because while he experienced the divorce as something bad happening to him (like a car accident), Rebecca experienced divorce as her own choice. Rebecca's mother sees it that way too, but she sees the choice to divorce as an admission of failure. Like many people, Rebecca's mother believes that all marriages have more or less the same positive and negative potential. She thinks that Rebecca's second marriage will be just as challenging and rewarding as her first, and that its "success" or "failure" will be determined by the character and skill of the participants. If Rebecca couldn't hold it together the first time around, what makes her think that it will be different the second time?

This is the golf game model of marriage, where everyone plays on the same course and only the most talented win. Unlike the car crash model of marriage, Rebecca is in control of the outcome. Since she spent her first game of golf trying to dig herself out of sand traps, the Cow predicts that she can't possibly win the next time around. Rebecca doesn't see it that way though; in her view, she was trying to play golf using a cantaloupe and a Wiffle ball bat in her first marriage. She does not believe that there was any way for her first marriage to have been successful, since she and Greg were simply a poor match for one another. In Rebecca's view, there is nothing fundamentally wrong with her or with Greg, and their divorce was not a mistake or the result of mistakes made along the way. She sees divorce as the most reasonable solution to the real mistake that she and Greg made, which was getting married in the first place.

Cultural attitudes towards second marriages are another indication that our society views divorce as a shameful public admission of defeat. The Holy Cow is pleased with these attitudes, and she is always looking for ways to perpetuate them. One of the best defenses against this Cow, like all of the Sacred Cows, is logic. We must press the Holy Cow to be perfectly clear on two points: Does the marriage contract require us to love one another forever, or does it require us to stay together forever even in the absence of love? Second, do we marry for love and the pursuit of happiness, or do we marry for the greater good of society? The Holy Cow may try to avoid the questions by mooing platitudes like "Love is not a feeling, it's a choice!" or "Your happiness comes from doing the right thing and from putting the good of other people ahead of your own good!" However, with gentle persistence, you can persuade her to show her cards. If she comes down on the side of love, then she has undermined her own arguments, because she can't possibly defend the position that love never dies. On the other hand, if she tells you that marriage is about economic and social stability, and that your happiness should take a backseat to the needs of society, you are free to tell her whether that's what you signed up for or not. Once you have disentangled the Holy Cow's claims that you can have it all ("You create your own love! You will be happier if you stop focusing on your own happiness!"), you will realize that she has been milking cultural clichés to create guilt and shame, and that is e*moo*tional manipulation.

> Any woman who votes for no-fault divorce is like a turkey voting for Thanksgiving.
>
> —Pat Robertson, *The 700 Club*

The Holy Cow as a political tool

The Holy Cow is ambitious, and she doesn't restrict her focus to individual marriages. She knows how to engage social and political forces for her cause, including the United States government. Marriage is promoted in the US by the government and religious organizations as a cornerstone for a stable and happy society. According to Fox News, under the second Bush administration, Congress allocated $750 million to programs aimed at preserving marriages. The money was mainly spent in public relations and advertising efforts aimed at educating Americans about how to navigate the treacherous waters of dating, engagement, marriage and child rearing. (Oddly, our politicians in Washington consider themselves experts in these arenas.) The theory is that since married parents are wealthier, healthier and have more advantaged children than single parents, it must be the act of marriage that has *caused* them to become wealthier and healthier. We can therefore solve the problems of poverty by convincing everyone to get married. (Perhaps we should stop shipping food to countries in crisis and start shipping marriage certificates instead.)

The flip side of encouraging marriage is discouraging divorce, but there is less political focus on programs specifically aimed at stopping divorce. There are likely many reasons for this, but one obvious reason is that rates for divorce have been declining since 1980 without any government interference whatsoever. Were you aware that divorce rates have been steadily decreasing for the past three decades? If you were not, this does not surprise us. There are many articles written in the popular press about marriage and divorce, but nearly all of them recycle the same "news" and get information from common sources.

Udderly Personal

For me there are two perspectives on divorce—that of the Dumper and that of the Dumpee. As the Dumpee I felt Sadness, Anger, and a dramatic loss of Self-esteem. I felt judged and found lacking, as if the divorce were something I could have/ should have prevented and could not because I was too flawed. The divorce also clashed dramatically with my sense of values. I was terribly bothered by the fact that we had made a commitment to each other "for better or for worse, until death do us part"—and it turned out that what he really meant was "until I change my mind, or until I decide on someone else," and now I was being asked to say that I agreed to this divorce.

—Sometimes Still Bitter in San Diego

One of the principal sources is the National Marriage Project, founded at Rutgers University in 1997 and now based at the University of Virginia. The stated goal of National Marriage Project is to "investigate how American marriages are formed, maintained and ended, and how society is affected." This sounds objective enough, until you discover that a core mission of this organization is to "identify strategies to increase marital quality and stability." Given that the goal of the organization is to promote marriage, it is understandable that all of their "findings" involve endorsements of marriage and dour warnings about the misery of divorce and single life. "Discoveries" by the National Marriage Project deliver on the expectations of its conservative funders such as the Templeton Foundation, and they are widely and uncritically reprinted by trusted news sources, helping to create the perspective that divorce rates are increasing and marriage is a solution to myriad social woes.

Divorce propaganda
and the popular press

According to Philip Cohen, professor of sociology at the University of Maryland, the reason that most divorce-related articles we read in the popular press derive from the National Marriage Project is that they have been very good at building a relationship with the news media. The National Marriage Project publishes an annual "The State of Our Unions" report that includes some marriage and divorce trends obtained from government reports, as well as a "5-page essay on the state of marriage, where they talk about the importance of marriage." According to Cohen, the media has become hooked on the annual report as a source of data, and newspapers gobble up the expertly written, pithy treatises issued by the National Marriage Project because they are a quick and cheap source of easily digested print.

Some examples of widely quoted nonsense about divorce are articles published between 2009 and 2012 claiming that economic recessions save marriage. (This and other examples can be found in Philip Cohen's blog *Family Inequality*.) In December 2009, an opinion article appeared in the *Wall Street Journal* summarizing the findings of *Money & Marriage*, a report by the National Marriage Project. The article was written by W. Bradford Wilcox, who happened to be the *director* of the National Marriage Project and a senior fellow at the Institute for American Values.

The article began by stating that the National Marriage Project had noted (or, as Wilcox should have written, "*we* noted") that financial pressures associated with the economic recession could result in marital stress. No big surprise there. The author went on to say that there may be a silver lining in all of the financial pain, however, because "For most married Americans, the Great Recession seems to be solidifying, not eroding, the marital bond. The divorce rate is actually falling. It declined to 16.9 divorces per 1,000 married women in 2008 from 17.5 divorces in 2007 (a 3% drop), after rising from 16.4 divorces per 1,000 married women in 2005 (a 7% increase)."

The writer mused for a moment about the possibility that some couples simply couldn't afford to get divorced and were postponing their divorce for better economic times. He then dismissed this idea in favor of "anecdotal evidence" suggesting that couples "have responded to the recession by re-dedicating themselves to their marriages." Based upon rather odd logic, Mr. Wilcox stated that thrift and meals at home were the cause of recession-strengthened marriages. The data he offered to support this statement were that couples without financial assets are 70% more likely to divorce than couples with $10,000 in financial assets.

So let's see if we can follow this: The recession causes job loss, which causes couples to use their credit cards less and to eat out less, which causes them to accumulate new wealth and assets. Now that they have more assets, they are less likely to divorce. Hmm. Well, if it's written in the *Wall Street Journal*, it must be true.

Mr. Wilcox then went on to state that the recession had

caused couples to abandon the "soul mate" model of marriage (i.e., the idea that marriage should be a source of emotional intimacy, sexual satisfaction and personal fulfillment) and rediscover good old-fashioned economic dependency. Or as he put it, "the value of a husband with a good health-care plan, a wife with a good job or in-laws who are willing to provide free child care or a temporary rent-free place to live." In other words, during the recession, American couples couldn't afford to get divorced.

The *Washington Times* referenced the same report by the National Marriage Project in their opinion section in May 2012. Janice Shaw Crouse wrote that the recession seemed to be solidifying the marital bond for "most couples," and that the divorce rate was falling because couples were learning to compromise and "stick it out."

USA Today had this to say about the same report in February 2011: "Exactly how many marriages have been saved is unknown, but the US divorce rate fell 7% between 2006 and 2009." Also, "The silver lining is that [the recession] seems to have deepened ties to one another and to the marriage" for many couples.

The *New York Times* agreed, quoting Mr. Wilcox as saying, "I think that deepened commitment will be there even after the economy improves."

The National Marriage Project report was all over the print media, widely disseminating the idea that economic recession significantly impacts divorce rates, at least in part because hard times bring couples closer. What the news media didn't tell us was that divorce rates have been in a steady decline for decades, through economic boom and bust. To illustrate this, look at the graph below of the crude divorce rate in the USA over the past three decades. As you can see, the clear trend is down. (The decline in the divorce rate per 1,000 married women has been less steep, in part because the marriage rate has also been declining, but the downward trend is the same.) We have circled for you the part of the graph that all of these news articles were referencing. Indeed, Mr. Wilcox was correct: After an increase in the rate of divorce in 2005, the divorce rate declined again. Looking at the graph, this hardly seems like a trend worth writing about, let alone reporting in every major newspaper in America.

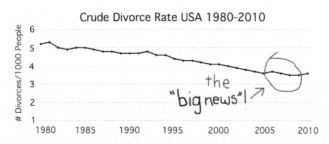

Crude Divorce Rate USA 1980-2010

The story was not just about a supposedly newsworthy decline in the US divorce rate, however, but also about the strengthening effect of economic recession on marriage. In order for you to compare the expansion and contraction of the US economy relative to the divorce rate, we have graphed both together and again circled the period of interest. As you can see, there is no obvious correlation between the change in real GDP and divorce rate. While an expert economist might be able to dig out some sort of complicated mathematical relationship between some aspects of the American economy and divorce rates, we think that you will agree that none of this looks very newsworthy.

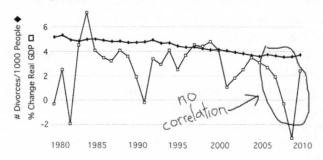

Change in Real GDP Compared with Divorce Rate 1980-2010

We have come up with our own divorce correlation, however, which we are very excited about. As you will see below, the rate of smoking among men in the USA was highly correlated with the divorce rate between 1980 and 2010! We considered the possibility that this is a coincidence, but we have thrown that possibility out in favor of anecdotal evidence that people don't like to kiss smokers. One of the many virtues of abstaining from tobacco smoking is the obvious effect it has on strengthening marriage. Probably a lot of women who would have divorced their spouses because of stinky cigarette breath are staying married to their now ex-smoking husbands. We are waiting by the phone for the calls from the *Wall Street Journal* and the *New York Times* about our exciting new scoop!

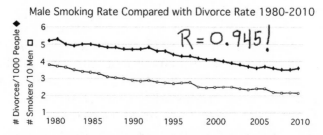

Male Smoking Rate Compared with Divorce Rate 1980-2010

Obviously, this is a silly example of correlation between two sets of statistics that are very likely unrelated. It is also a ridiculous example of how easy it is to make up a story of causation between two unrelated variables. However, we think that it is no more ridiculous than what the papers actually printed about divorce and economic recession. Even opinion pages should not be that sloppy.

Happy countries

We started this discussion about the politics of marriage and divorce by highlighting political concern about the falling prevalence of marriage in our society. The reason for concern by organizations such as the Institute for American Values (sponsor of the National Marriage Project) is the belief that marriage creates a wealthier and more stable society. Rates of single parenthood and divorce are high in poorer segments of

American society compared with wealthier segments, and other features of social instability, such as crime rates, are also more common in poorer neighborhoods.

Conservative groups in this country have made the rash leap from correlation to causation, concluding that marriage causes wealth and social stability. They could equally have concluded that wealth and social stability create marriage, but that conclusion would have left them with a conundrum: encouraging marriage among poor people would involve wealth transfer, which is not a popular idea with the sort of people who are concerned about increasing marriage prevalence.

Let's look at the first conclusion, then, that marriage causes wealth and stability. On the micro (personal) scale, this appears to be true, because running a single household is less expensive than running two, and having two adults in a home generally creates flexibility. If we expand our logic from "two can live more cheaply than one" to the national scale, countries with high marriage prevalence should be wealthier, happier and more stable than countries with low marriage prevalence.

Let's take examples at both ends of the spectrum and see how this plays out. A country with both a low marriage rate and high divorce rate is Sweden, where more children are born out of wedlock than to married couples. By contrast, divorce rates in Libya are tenfold lower than in Sweden (and nearly fifteenfold lower than the United States), and marriage rates are significantly higher than in the US or Sweden. Yet this difference has not translated into some of the expected social benefits. According to a Gallup World Poll, Sweden is the fourth happiest country in the world, and Libya is 67th. According to the World Bank, Sweden is the 13th richest country in the world in terms of purchasing power parity per capita, and Libya is 56th despite large oil reserves. Murder is several times as common in Libya than in Sweden, and we are all aware of how much political unrest Libyans have suffered recently. Would anyone suggest that pushing more Swedes into marriage would achieve the sort of social nirvana enjoyed in Libya? If we are unwise enough to impute causation, then the facts would suggest the opposite: that we should encourage more Libyans to divorce to improve *their* national happiness. We should therefore be skeptical when the Holy Cow claims that by increasing marriage prevalence in America, we will create a wealthier, happier and more stable country.

Commitment good, pain bad

Two very good reasons to avoid divorce are that it is painful and it involves breaking a commitment. In general, most of us would agree that pain is bad and commitment is good for the individual and for society. Yet neither pain nor commitment breaking by itself should be a legitimate *unilateral* reason for calling something bad. If your mother committed to giving all of her earthly assets to a church that you thought was a scary cult, you would probably encourage her to break that commitment. Similarly, if your brother were afraid of gut-wrenching withdrawal as a result of quitting his heroin habit, you would still encourage him to quit and go through the pain. In the same way, merely knowing that divorce is painful or that divorce involves the breaking of a commitment is not *by itself* sufficient reason to discourage someone you love from seeking a divorce. On the flip side, the knowledge that weddings involve making commitments and eating cake is not by itself enough reason to encourage someone to wed.

The holy last word

The Bible condemns divorce, but as the United States remains primarily a Christian nation, it is worth pointing out that Jesus was not much of a family man himself. He pushed his mother away, and he never married. He asked his followers to abandon their families to be with him. In fact, Jesus said, "Assuredly, I say to you, there is no one who has left house or parents or brothers or wife or children, for the sake of the kingdom of God, who shall not receive many times more in this present time, and in the age to come eternal life." Jesus had his reasons, probably, and we do not presume to question them. In fact, we will leave you with these words from Jesus himself to end our Holy Cow discussion: "Judge not, and you will not be judged; condemn not, and you will not be condemned; forgive, and you will be forgiven."

CHAPTER TWO
The Expert Cow

Marriage counselors know the secret to a long marriage:
never get divorced.
—*Anonymous*

Meet the Cow

The Expert Cow is a bossy bovine. She shows up when you are at your most vulnerable and uses a mantle of authority to push her agenda. Before she even meets you, she has made up her mind about what you need and how you should try to get it. She may have a financial stake in a therapeutic technique that she has invented, or she may just have a pet theory that she believes applies to everybody. She claims that her views are scientifically accurate, even though there's nothing  to back her claims. Be on the lookout for this huckster Cow loitering in the offices of marriage counselors and between the pages of relationship self-help books.

Caveat: The Expert Cow does not represent all marriage counselors or all self-help books. Many wise, helpful professionals do real good for couples in distress. This Sacred Cow shows up when the expert is more interested in his or her own dogma or financial reward than in the happiness of vulnerable people seeking help, or when the expert fails to recognize or disclose his or her limitations or biases.

Spotting the Expert Cow

At some point in nearly every distressed relationship, the question of couples counseling arises. There are many types of counseling out there, and many types of counselors, and we are wholly unqualified to give advice about what sort might be right for you. We feel fully qualified, however, to stalk Sacred Cows in all of their habitats, be they therapists' offices or on the pages of self-help books. These Sacred Cows can be an impediment to progress towards greater happiness, and we hope to offer you the tools for spotting these Cows and for gently tipping them over when they get in the way of informed decisions.

Marriage counseling Q & A

Does marriage therapy work?

Excellent question. We must, however, request that you rephrase your question to be more specific.

Is there scientific evidence that marriage therapy prevents divorce?

No, that question has never effectively been studied.

Is there scientific evidence that marriage therapy helps people in troubled marriages to sort out whether they should stay married?

See #2 above.

Is there scientific evidence that marriage therapy will make my marriage more fulfilling?

See #2 above.

Can marriage therapy improve anything?

Ah, we are glad that you asked. Yes, probably. According to

a Meta-Analytic Review of Marital Therapy Outcome Research, there is good evidence that it can improve your GARQ.

What on earth is a GARQ?

You don't know? And you're married? No *wonder* you are confused!

Um, could you please answer my question?

The GARQ is the General Assessment of the Relationship and Its Quality Measures. It is also called the Dyadic Adjustment Scale.

Could you please answer my question like you actually want me to understand you?

The GARQ is a scale used to measure marital distress. It was built from a bunch of existing questionnaires about relationship satisfaction and then administered to 218 white, married people (in person) and 94 recently divorced people (by mail … presumably it was hard to get them in a room together). The scale is considered accurate, as it consistently distinguishes distressed from non-distressed couples.

Thanks a lot. I already know that my spouse and I are "distressed." I don't need a GARQ to tell me that.

Yes, but our point was that marriage counseling could improve your GARQ.

So if I fill out this questionnaire before marriage counseling and then again after marriage counseling, I am likely to have a higher score the second time?

Seems so.

If my spouse and I improve our scores, does that mean that we are happier?

Well, there are 32 questions on this particular questionnaire. Some questions ask how often you and your spouse agree about various topics, such as finances or in-laws. Others ask about how often you fight and how much you enjoy each other's company. Question 31 asks if you are happy. If you answer question

31 with a higher score the second time around, then you are presumably happier.

Does this mean that marriage counseling will help us to have a more satisfying lifelong relationship?

Well, we don't really know.

Then what does all this mean??

It means that there *is* evidence that marriage counseling can help some couples to feel better. There is no reliable evidence, however, that marriage counseling saves doomed marriages or can fix your specific problems. So go to a marriage counselor if you think it might help you, but don't let people bully you into going—or into continuing—if you know that your problems are not the sort that can be helped by a therapist.

The Marriage Fairy

Of course, knowing whether your problems can be fixed by marriage counseling is no easy matter. Most people want to explore every option before taking the painful step of dissolving a marriage, and a visit to a counselor is a worthy venture. This venture can backfire, however, when the expectations and agendas of all involved parties are not placed openly on the table. Anxiety, anger and grief that accompany marital instability can make it hard to think straight, and desperate need for a solution makes people vulnerable to incompetent, ill-suited or mercenary therapists. This is where the Marriage Fairy might come in handy.

As a first step before seeking marriage counseling, it is useful for distressed couples to examine their basic desires. Imagine that the Marriage Fairy has appeared with her magic wand, offering to make your wish come true. She will magically fulfill your greatest desire about your marriage. (She doesn't grant wishes about money or eternal life; she is the *Marriage* Fairy.) What do you ask her for? Nobody else will know that you made a wish, so you can be perfectly honest. Do you ask the fairy to wave her wand to cause your spouse to agree with you about how to raise the kids, how to spend the money, or whether your mother is a reasonable person? Do you ask her to enchant your spouse so that every evening he or she will amorously pull you into the bedroom the moment you walk through the door? Do you ask her to cast a spell on you so that your heart will be filled with love for your spouse? Or do you ask her to cause your spouse to fall in love with the tennis pro and run off to Brazil?

Once you are able to identify your basic desire or most fervent wish for your marriage, you will be better equipped to select the most appropriate tools for addressing your problems. Marriages can be unhappy for many reasons, which is why one-size-fits-all marital advice is rarely helpful. If you are wildly attracted to your spouse but are coming to the painful conclusion that he or she is a self-absorbed unsupportive person, then you may not benefit from advice about rekindling passion. On the other hand, if

---

Udderly Personal

I suspect that my wife and I went to couples therapy too late, once our relationship was already beyond repair. I found the therapist useful only for mediating conversations with my ex and for providing a safe forum where I could open up without reservation. I don't think that the therapist provided any real help for our relationship, however.

I don't believe that there's any way to prospectively figure out whether a counselor will be a good fit for a couple or whether therapy will help a relationship. It is not easy to find a good therapist, but most importantly, couples often get to therapy too late. If I could share one piece of advice, it would be to find a tool to maintain connectedness and stoke the fire of passion in marriage long before real problems emerge. Also, I found that individual therapy was helpful for me during the process of divorce, when I had to work on self-healing and consistency in my relationship with my ex regardless of the state of my own emotions. So even if marriage counseling doesn't help you, don't give up on therapy in general; it can sometimes be useful.

—Wiser in Wisconsin

---

your spouse is a nice person but there's just not enough love left to keep your marriage glued together, you're not going to get much out of conflict resolution training. Until you examine your own reasons for considering divorce, you won't be able to tell your therapist how to help you. More importantly, you won't be able to recognize when the problem you are having is beyond the reach of self-help books, counselors and therapists. Sadly, not every problem has a solution. Yet there are many experts out there who are ready to offer advice (for a fee), even if that advice is completely tangential to your real problem. It is a rare professional who will say, "Yours is the sort of problem that cannot be solved even by my sagest advice."

What is the job of a marriage counselor?

One of the reasons to define your goals for therapy is to avoid choosing the wrong resource. Most marriage counselors and books are oriented towards the goals of reducing conflict and rekindling romance, and if your problems do not lie in these realms, counseling can be a demoralizing waste of time and money. Even worse is the situation where one spouse's basic desire is to be out of the marriage when the other spouse has not been informed or is not accepting of that fact. If the therapist does not bring in the Marriage Fairy to sort out what both spouses really want, then the whole exercise can become absurd. Let's do a thought experiment to imagine how this could play out.

Justine and Antoine have been married for ten years. When they met, Antoine was captivated by Justine's high spirits and warm, adventurous personality. Antoine was just the sort of responsible, kind, nurturing man Justine had been seeking, and they happily committed to a life together. They had children early and enjoyed parenting together. In every detail, their relationship appeared perfect. Slowly, however, it dawned on Justine that she and Antoine were spending more and more time apart. They had separate hobbies and even sometimes took separate vacations. Antoine never spontaneously kissed her, and sex had become perfunctory and unsatisfying. As Justine became increasingly unhappy in her marriage, she requested that they seek marriage counseling. Antoine was reluctant at first, but then confessed that he was also unhappy and willing to try to find a solution.

After listening to Antoine and Justine's description of their problems, the marriage counselor began (as she did with all of her clients) by teaching them about empathetic listening, a fundamental skill for any successful relationship. They were first taught to use "I" messages as the speaker.

"I feel that we have drifted apart over the years, Antoine," said Justine.

"I admit that I don't feel close to you anymore," replied Antoine.

"I want to have the sort of relationship where you are happy to be around me and eager to hold my hand while we sit together like this!"

"I want that too!" responded Antoine in a choked voice. "I love you so much. But I feel like I just can't please you. You always seem annoyed with me. I feel like I'm failing you!"

"But I don't feel that way at all!" replied a surprised Justine. "What makes you think this?"

"Every time I do anything around the house, you feel the need to 'fix' it, like I'm incompetent. Every time I try to talk to you about things that matter to me, you get impatient. You never ask me about my day at work, and I assume that you just don't care. You don't trust me to take care of the kids, and yet you constantly complain that you do all of the work!"

The therapist reminded Antoine that he was supposed to be using "I" statements, and Justine and Antoine spent the next several sessions talking through long-neglected issues. They ultimately ironed out most of their misunderstandings and regained a happy relationship. They commented often over the years about how helpful marriage counseling had been for them.

Now let's imagine a different scenario where lack of

communication was not the major issue. We are back in the therapist's office in this alternate universe with Antoine and Justine, and Justine says:

"I feel that we have drifted apart over the years, Antoine."

"I admit that I don't feel close to you anymore," replied Antoine.

"I want to have the sort of relationship where you are happy to be around me and eager to hold my hand while we sit together like this!"

"I'm afraid that I won't be able to give you what you want," responded Antoine in a choked voice. "I don't think that I love you anymore, and I don't believe I can make myself be in love just by trying harder."

"I don't know what to say to that," replied Justine.

There was an awkward pause, and the therapist moved on to the next chapter in her syllabus, "Being a Good Listener by Reflecting."

"I'm not in love with you anymore, and I don't believe I can make myself be in love just by trying harder," said Antoine.

"I hear you saying that you don't think that you are in love with me anymore, that you want to be my friend but you no longer want to be my lover," replied Justine.

"That's right, you have heard what I was trying to tell you. I respect you and care for you, but I no longer have romantic feelings towards you."

Both Antoine and Justine began to cry, so the therapist moved on to chapter 3 in her syllabus, "Validating."

"I'm not in love with you anymore, and I don't believe I can make myself be in love just by trying harder," said Antoine.

"I now understand that you have not really loved me for many years, and that explains why you have increasingly built your life around your work and your friends. I realize that we have spent more and more time apart even within our own home, which makes sense if you don't love me anymore," replied Justine.

Both of them began to cry again. The therapist moved on to the final chapter in her syllabus, "Empathizing."

"I'm not in love with you anymore, and I don't believe I can make myself be in love just by trying harder," said Antoine.

"I understand how upsetting it must be for you to be married to someone you don't think you really love anymore. Truly, I understand how tortured you feel right now." Justine dissolved into tears.

Since listening exercises clearly weren't making the couple any happier, the therapist decided to try some exercises to build intimacy. She assigned the couple a romantic dinner and an evening of looking through photos of happier times. The evening ended with a fight in the restaurant; Justine accused Antoine of making her feel humiliated by his lack of feeling, and Antoine told her angrily that he wasn't doing it on purpose.

The therapist then assigned Antoine to write three things he likes or admires about Justine every day. After a month, he had made a long list of positive statements, but it hadn't changed how he felt. The therapist told him that he should act like he was in love with Justine and the feeling would follow, but that led to more accusations from Justine about his lack of sincerity and worsening feelings of inadequacy and self-loathing for Antoine. Finally, Antoine burst out in anger during a counseling session, saying that nobody was listening to him about the fact that he couldn't change his feelings at will, and he was tired of the browbeating. He stormed out of the office, leaving Justine in tears (again).

In this situation, Antoine and Justine likely did benefit from couples counseling because it forced them to have an important conversation about how Antoine felt. However, once that point had been reached, further empathetic listening exercises were pointless. The therapist was following her syllabus because it was the program she used for all of her married clients, but it was a waste of Justine and Antoine's money and time. Worse, it made Antoine feel unnecessarily guilty and inadequate when the fixes prescribed by the counselor didn't work.

The Expert Cow reared her head when the therapist failed to have a conversation with Justine and Antoine about their goals and acknowledge that she might not have a solution.

Reasonable people could disagree about whether or not therapy can help someone to fall in love again, but Antoine was pretty certain that it wasn't going to happen. A direct conversation about this subject would have helped Justine and Antoine to make better decisions.

The therapist did not bring up the subject of divorce, which is not uncommon; some counselors take the position that divorce constitutes a failure by all parties involved, including the therapist. These therapists see themselves as marriage saviors and are therefore not well equipped to help clients to sort out whether they would be happier together or apart. Analogously, imagine that your son complains to you about being unhappy at school. You sincerely want to make him feel better, but you are not going to discuss with him the possibility that school may not be for him. You have already decided that dropping out of school is a failure, and so you will do your best to convince him to ride out the tough parts as an investment in his future happiness.

In the same way, a marriage counselor who sees divorce as a failure is not going to help you explore the possibility of divorce. This is fine as long as you are wholly committed to staying in your marriage. In fact, if you know that divorce is not an acceptable outcome for you, it's possibly better to seek a therapist who believes in saving marriages at any cost. Antoine, however, had a voice in the back of his mind telling him that divorce might be the best solution. Avoidance of the subject during therapy reinforced his sense that divorce is a failure and increased his feelings of shame and frustration. Antoine should have started the first conversation with the therapist by asking, "Do you see it as your most important job to help me and Justine become happier people or to save the marriage?"

The Expert Cow in print

In the same way, most books written for people in unhappy marriages will start out by promising a happier marriage. The very titles promise marriage salvation, such as *We Can Work It*

Out: How to Solve Conflicts, Save Your Marriage, and Strengthen Your Love for Each Other and *Why Marriages Succeed or Fail: And How You Can Make Yours Last.* If you pick up a book like that hoping to sort out whether staying married is the best choice for you, you will read that of course it is! That message is so strong in these books that issues that could (or maybe should) be deal breakers in a marriage are seldom raised. For instance, you are likely to find a list pretty early on in these books that is meant to help you diagnose your marriage problems. The list will look something like this:

True or False:
- My spouse and I often argue about money.
- We have frequent arguments about in-laws.
- We cannot agree about the assignment of household chores.
- I feel that my spouse does not show me enough affection.
- We have disagreements about sex.
- When we have arguments, one of us usually walks away.
- My spouse does not understand me.
- I do not feel supported by my spouse.

After answering a battery of such questions, you add up your score and find out either that your marriage is not in trouble after all (phew!) or it needs some work (boo!), but reading the book can make it better (phew!).

Here are the questions that you will seldom find in these lists:

- Do you no longer love your spouse?
- Are you in a physically or emotionally abusive relationship?
- Do you feel that your spouse is not a good or admirable person?
- Do you believe that your spouse no longer loves you?
- Do you suspect that your spouse is gay (and you are not) or your spouse is straight (and you are not)?

- Do you think that your spouse is fundamentally incapable of real intimacy and that you are doomed to a life of loneliness if you stay married to this person?
- Do you find your spouse sexually unappealing?
- Did you get to the end of all of these questions only to find that your score indicates your marriage is just fine, but you have an empty feeling in your heart that you fear can never be filled?

The reason that these questions aren't usually on the list is that there's no obvious solution to these problems. Or rather, the only reasonable solution might sometimes be to get a divorce. This is where the Sacred Cow is hiding: By failing to acknowledge

Udderly Personal

When my husband and I were on the brink of divorce, our counselor advised us to attend a retreat organized by famous psychologists who had written a popular self-help book. We were invited to spend a few days (and about $6000) hiking, skiing and attending intensive marital therapy in a halcyon mountain retreat. I called the organizers to get a sense of what to expect. In five minutes, I summarized the bare bones of the problems that we were facing. "Ah yes!" said the famous psychologist. "I can see that you have the most common problem: an adolescent approach to sexuality. If you come to our retreat, I believe that we will be able to save your marriage. We have a very high success rate!"

"But," I thought, "we didn't even discuss the subject of sexuality … How could she possibly diagnose this?" I concluded that either this famous psychologist was the Annie Oakley of psychology, able to predict marital success in five minutes from 2000 miles away, or she had some very expensive Snake Oil Liniment to Cure What Ails You. People in desperate situations are easy prey for those who offer miracle cures at great expense. We did not attend the retreat.

—Cynical in Cincinnati

that these problems could be present, the experts who write these books are pushing readers to focus on what might be red herrings. All of the conflict resolution training in the world isn't going to change the fact that your spouse has an incompatible sexual orientation, doesn't love you, or has a personality disorder with which you cannot come to terms. And yet these books (and many counselors) take couples through formulaic steps meant to address a problem that the couple doesn't really have, while at the same time ignoring the problem that the couple really does have. This can lead to confusion, feelings of failure, or worst of all, efforts to achieve enlightenment by reading oddball books about Sacred Cows and GARQs.

Marriage counselors aren't gods

As the American sportscaster Vin Scully observed, "Statistics are used much like a drunk uses a lamppost: for support, not illumination." Experts love to tell us about statistics and scientific "facts." What experts often fail to mention is that there are hard facts and soft facts. Hard facts are demonstrably true, or testable, whereas soft facts are speculative. An example of a hard fact would be that kids who have access to guidance counselors go to college at higher rates than kids without such access. An example of a soft fact would be that guidance counselors help get kids get into college. That second one is a soft fact because there might be some other reason the hard fact is true, like rich kids at good schools have guidance counselors and poor kids at bad schools don't. Just as many rich kids might have gone to college even if every guidance counselor in the country called in sick for a year.

The analogy to marriage counseling should be clear: divorce research is overwhelmingly about soft facts. There are lots of good reasons for this, but probably the biggest reason is that large, well-designed studies simply do not exist in this field. Governments and big companies do not fund family research in the same way that they fund medical and applied science research;

consequently, family research is a cottage industry in the United States.[1] Even meta-analyses of marriage counseling studies (papers that try to summarize all of the research in a particular area) include unpublished graduate student dissertations and non-peer-reviewed studies, something that is unheard of in most scientific fields.[2] Most published studies about divorce are small, observational in nature, and rife with bias. When we asked Philip Cohen, a professor of sociology who specializes in family research, about definitive studies related to divorce, he said, "The idea of a definitive study is probably going to be elusive because we don't have the longitudinal data to do that. If you really want to do it right, you need to follow people from beginning to end. Lots of people try to approximate that with various sorts of research designs, but it's difficult. I don't think you're going to find a definitive study."

We did look for a definitive study, but we could not find a single research paper about the long-term effectiveness of marriage counseling that, had the study been performed on a new drug candidate, would have received anything other than laughter from evaluators at the Federal Drug Administration. There are understandable reasons for this. As mentioned above, it is expensive to follow couples over long periods of time, and so collecting data on divorce rates after an intervention like marriage counseling would require a lot of *moo*lah. Also, to determine whether marriage counseling prevents divorce, subjects would need to be randomly assigned to counseling or to no counseling. If a couple said, "We are in real trouble and we think we need marriage counseling," it would be hard to argue the ethics of randomly placing that couple in a no-counseling group. Even if counseling has no impact on divorce rates, it may be an important gateway for people to receive treatment for problems like anxiety, depression or substance abuse, and it could therefore be construed as unethical to deny access to counseling once requested. Furthermore, just because a couple gets assigned to a "no-counseling" group doesn't mean that they won't go get counseling somewhere else if they decide that they want it.

The fact that there are no randomized (i.e., picked without any kind of bias) prospective (i.e., started before anyone divorces) trials examining the impact of couples counseling on divorce rates means that nobody can make a plausible claim that couples counseling saves marriages. Books and counselors will claim to have an effective method to prevent divorce, but the bottom line is that nobody really knows, since the subject hasn't been studied in a fashion that could be considered, even remotely, to be rigorous.

Helpful tip: If you already get the point about research and you want to avoid more talk about studies, you can skip the next two sections. If you are gleefully rubbing your hands together at the prospect of examining some scientific claims, read on.

Although there are no randomized trials examining the long-term effectiveness of marriage counseling for couples in distress, we were able to identify one lone randomized trial in a related area. This German trial published in 2010 addresses the long-term effects of preventive behavioral therapy for married couples,[3] and it was the only study we could find that attempted a rigorous randomized, longitudinal design. In the context of this study, "preventative" means that these couples had not self-identified as needing therapy, but they were offered classes to learn how to communicate better with one another. We have chosen to describe this study in some detail here in order to illustrate the ways in which flawed scientific approaches can invalidate results, and how the authors' interpretations of their own studies can be misleading. This study is also a good example of the general state of marriage research: while the authors should be applauded for attempting a more rigorous randomized, longitudinal trial design, the final product falls far short of what would be considered valid in other disciplines.

For this randomized study, couples were invited to attend "communication seminars" designed to assist couples before problems developed. A total of 81 couples made it through the pre-assessment phase involving questionnaires, but 12 of these couples dropped out, refusing to proceed any further with the study. The remaining couples were randomized to either the learning program (31 couples) or a waiting list (36 couples). (Yes, these numbers are not equal as we would expect for randomization; we are puzzled also.) So far, aside from the small sample size and weird randomization numbers, it sounds pretty good: *Almost* half of couples randomly assigned to "communication seminars" could be compared with slightly more than half assigned to the waiting list. This should be a pretty fair comparison.

The intervention couples attended a weekend seminar of lectures and one-on-one communication exercises with a trainer. The wait-listed control group did what you would expect: wait. Ah, but it gets more complicated! The couples on the waiting list were offered the same weekend seminars as the intervention group, and 27 of the 36 couples opted to participate. The investigators included this group that crossed over from the waiting list in their analysis of seminar attendees. This makes sense, in a way, because now that they have had the same training as the intervention group, they can't very well serve as controls. The control group was then whittled down to the 9 couples who refused to participate in the seminar. Presumably since these were too few couples to analyze, the investigators threw in the 12 couples who had refused to participate outright in the very beginning. Eleven years later, the authors followed up to see how the groups had fared. They couldn't track down everyone, but they were able to compare 51 couples who had agreed to the seminars with 19 couples who had refused to attend the seminars. Yes: they "randomized" couples to different treatments and then completely ignored their own randomization to compare the one-third of couples unwilling or unable to participate in a communication seminar with the two-thirds who agreed to participate. Do you imagine that there might be differences between these two groups at baseline? Might the refusing couples have had more conflict, more life stresses, or poorer connectedness? Might you expect them to be at higher risk of divorce? We think so too. And what did the investigators find? (Drumroll, please …)

After eleven years, a higher percentage of non-seminar attendees were divorced than seminar attendees (though for the math inclined out there, this was only statistically significant if a one-tailed t-test was employed, and perhaps not even then as the p value is stated in one part of the paper to equal 0.024 and in another 0.24). There were no significant differences in how each group rated relationship satisfaction. When asked, "Do you remember any of the specific skills which were taught to you during the training?" fewer than half of respondents could remember a single skill. The authors wondered how skills that nobody could remember could prevent divorce, and postulated, "Maybe they employ their skills in everyday life without recognizing that the skills were taught to them?" Hmm, yes, maybe. But certainly when you compare couples eager to participate in a communication seminar with couples unwilling to participate, you can end up drawing completely erroneous conclusions about the value of your "intervention"!

Marriage gurus aren't gods either

Alongside the American cottage industry of family research lies the more lucrative and popular "marriage guru" industry. This industry is made up of individuals who have created brands around their ideas about marriage and use their brands to sell books, seminars, lectures, and sometimes individual couples therapy. One of the best-known marriage gurus in America is John Gottman from the University of Washington. Gottman has created an empire based upon what he calls "breakthrough research" and "scientific direct observations published in peer-reviewed literature." He is famous for claiming to be able to predict which couples will divorce and which will stay happily together after listening to them talk for as little as five minutes. Good marketing has made him a minor celebrity, and you may have read about his work in the press or in Malcolm Gladwell's popular book *Blink*. Part of what makes Gottman's claim so seductive to journalists and writers is that he offers highly precise and impressive numbers for the accuracy of his predictions. In his book *The Seven Principles for Making Marriage Work*, Gottman claims to be able to predict whether a couple will divorce with 91% accuracy. That seems astounding, like something out of science fiction. Imagine if you could go to a fortune-teller with a question such as "Will I meet the man I am going to marry this year?" and you knew that she would get the answer wrong only 9% of the time. That would be a fortune-teller worth a fortune, for sure.

You may be thinking that predicting divorce with high accuracy is a good way for a fortune-teller to make money, but a lousy way for a marriage guru to make money. If Gottman tells you that you are going to get divorced, you will probably decide to save the money you would have spent on his expensive retreats and workshops to pay your lawyer instead. Not so fast! Gottman claims that by scientifically discovering what causes marriages to fail, he has crafted a highly effective set of principles that will save your marriage. Let's look at how this works.

Gottman and his colleagues study couples in what has been dubbed the "Love Lab." The real innovation in his approach to marriage research is that he has developed the means to characterize and quantify emotional reactions of couples interacting in real time. Couples are invited to discuss an issue that they have identified as one of the most contentious in their marriage. The couple's interaction is captured on videotape that is later viewed and scored using specific codes. The coders watch facial expression and body posture, listen to tone of voice and assign a term for each segment of the video from a list of positive and negative behaviors and emotions. Examples include interest, validation, affection, disgust, belligerence, defensiveness or sadness. Heart rate and skin conductance are also monitored and analyzed. This approach theoretically reduces bias by adding a layer of objectivity, and it also yields the sort of data that can be quantified and analyzed statistically, making it more "scientific."

The study that propelled Gottman to fame was published

in 1998. In this study, Gottman and colleagues recruited 130 newlywed couples to come to the Love Lab for observation, and then annually reported their level of marital satisfaction for somewhere between three to six years, depending on when they entered the study. The goal was to figure out what features of newlywed interactions predicted who would get divorced during the years of follow-up. In this study, seventeen couples ended up divorced. The investigators then chose groups from the remaining married couples for comparison with the seventeen divorced couples.

When Gottman and his team crunched their data, they announced that they could predict with an "astounding" 83% accuracy which couples would divorce! The announcement spread like wildfire through the popular press after the research journal hired a publicist to help in disseminating the findings to the media.

Only, as Laurie Abraham pointed out elegantly in an article for *Slate*, Gottman and his group hadn't predicted anything. All they had done was look at who was divorced and not divorced, and then tease out which of their variables correlated with each state. In all of the decades of Love Lab research, nobody has tested the actual predictive ability of their formula. To do this, they would need to recruit a new group of newlyweds, make their measurements and place their bet on the table for everyone to see. Then three to six years later, we could all look back at the initial bet to see if they were right.

There are good reasons why nobody has tried this (or, alternatively, tried it and didn't report the poor results). The biggest problem is that what Gottman and his group did is plagued by a problem called "overfitting." Overfitting can result in a formula that looks great on paper but performs dismally in real life. A second problem is that the word "accuracy" can be misleading in the context of tests applied to human populations. Scientists talk about the sensitivity and specificity of a test (how many positives and negatives the test can identify) and about positive and negative predictive value (how many of the positives and negatives are true positives and negatives). You can't call a test "accurate" unless all of these numbers look good. To see how these statistical traps mess us up, let's look at some analogies.

Imagine that you have looked at dozens of variables that you thought might affect the outcome of professional football games. You gathered data on weather patterns, distance players traveled, athletes' diets, volume of the coach's voice, number of pets owned by the team manager, etc., etc. You analyzed all of the past Super Bowl games, and you came up with a group of variables that were associated 83% of the time with a particular team winning. It's easy to imagine that if you looked at enough variables, you would find some through random chance that seemed to correlate with wins and losses. In fact, if you studied enough variables, you can pretty much *guarantee* finding something that correlates perfectly. It's possible, for instance, that 83% of the time when it rained during the game, the team from farthest north won. Or 83% of the time when the quarterback ate a pork product the day before the game, that team lost. But if you tell your friends that if it rains, you can predict the outcome of the next Super Bowl game with 83% accuracy, your friends will laugh at you until you have successfully proven that you can deliver on this promise year after year.

What you did by selecting one variable out of many variables that correlate with a particular event (Super Bowl wins) is overfit. This problem is exacerbated when you are studying a small number of subjects to predict an event that is relatively rare. Let's say that when you examined all of the last 47 Super Bowl games, you discovered that every time the Cowboys play the Buffalo Bills, the Cowboys win. You could claim to be able to predict a Cowboys win next time this same matchup occurs, but your friends would just laugh at you again. They know that just because something happened twice doesn't mean that it will happen again. Similarly, if you take low numbers of divorces (like 17) and identify a trend that is present 83% of the time (i.e., in 14 divorces), there's a significant probability that what you have discovered is only a fluke.

To understand the importance of positive and negative

predictive value, let's use another example. In the late 1980s, there was a lot of fear about HIV, and some regions in the country mandated HIV testing for anyone applying for a marriage license. Let's say for the sake of our example that the test for HIV back then could accurately identify who was HIV infected 98% of the time and who was not infected with the virus 98% of the time (or in other words, was 98% sensitive and specific). That sounds like a really great test, doesn't it? Even better than Gottman's divorce predictor.

However, the rate of HIV infection among people applying for marriage licenses was very low, around 1 in 10,000. If the HIV test was wrong 2% of the time, then by testing 10,000 people you would probably find the one person infected with HIV, but you would also tell 200 other people that they had HIV when in fact they did not. It doesn't look like such an accurate test anymore, does it?

In response to the 1998 Gottman paper, researchers Richard Heyman and Amy Smith Slep created a model to show the effects of overfitting and positive predictive value in action. They developed a predictive equation for divorce in one sample population and then tried to cross-validate the equation in another sample. An equation with an initial overall "accuracy" of 90% ended up with a positive predictive value of 21%.[4] It is interesting that these valid critiques did not diminish the enthusiasm with which the news media continued to report Gottman's findings. Perhaps we all want to believe that somebody out there can tell us our fortune and be right.

After that long-winded discussion of statistics, we have only addressed the issue of whether Gottman's formula can predict divorce. We have not even touched on his more important claim that he possesses a formula that can save marriages. Has he even attempted to prove that his relationship advice has an impact on divorce rates? Of course not. He doesn't need to. If you're interested in the subject of marriage, chances are excellent that you already own his book. It is sitting on our bookshelf too.

Just because it isn't scientific doesn't mean it's bad

The point of the preceding arguments is not that marriage counselors and marriage self-help books have no value. Many of the things we value do not come backed with scientific proof. We don't need a scientist to tell us that a vacation in Hawaii is likely to make us happier; we can go and find out for ourselves. Similarly, if you think that going to a therapist or reading *The Seven Principles for Making Marriage Work* will make you feel better and/or improve your relationship, by all means do it. You may gain new insights, and it could cause you and your spouse to feel happier. Maybe it could even save your marriage … Although there's no scientific evidence to prove that books and counseling prevent divorce, there's no strong evidence that they *don't* prevent divorce either.

What we hope to achieve by examining some of the scientific claims backing up marriage advice is merely to equip you to spot the Sacred Cows. If you feel that you are being bullied into attending therapy sessions or reading books you don't want, you now have the ability to question the rationale for why you need to comply. A nice thing about Sacred Cows is that exposure to the bright light of critical questioning usually causes them to wander away.

How happy are you?

Do you remember the GARQ, or Dyadic Adjustment Scale we referenced at the beginning of this chapter? That is the questionnaire that can be used to measure the quality of a marriage or level of distress in a couple. Well, we have created our own Marriage Official Objective Scale (MOO Scale) that we think will perform just as well:

Question 1: What year did you get married?
Question 2: Which side of the bed do you sleep on?

Question 3: Do you like peanut butter?

Question 4: Are you taller than your spouse?

Question 5: The dots on the following line represent different degrees of happiness in your relationship. The number 3 point, "happy," represents the average degree of happiness of relationships. Please circle the dot that best describes the degree of happiness, all things considered, of your relationship.

```
0 -------- 1 -------- 2 -------- 3 -------- 4 -------- 5 -------- 6
```

| extremely unhappy | fairly unhappy | a little unhappy | happy | very happy | extremely happy | perfect |

Question 6: If you were stranded on a desert island with your spouse and could only bring one pet, one book, one bottle of wine, and one SUV, which of each would you pick?

Question 7: What color are your eyes?

Question 8: Do you think Brad Pitt or Angelina Jolie is hotter? Be honest.

Scoring:

If you like peanut butter, sleep on the left side of the bed and are taller than your spouse, give yourself a point if you were married in a prime- numbered year. Otherwise, give yourself two points. If you wondered how "side of the bed" is defined, multiply your score by two.

Give yourself one point for blue eyes, two points for green eyes and three points for brown eyes.

Give yourself three points for Brad Pitt. He's hotter. No contest.

Give yourself 1000 points for each point on the scale in question five. So if you circled number 4, that's 4000 points for you.

Question 6 is a trick. Take a point away if you listed any SUV to take to a desert island.

Add up all your points.

If you have over 3000 points, there's a good chance that your marriage will be okay. If you have fewer than 2000 points, then your marriage is in distress.

Explanation:

As you probably noticed, this quiz is just a sneaky, roundabout way of asking you whether or not you are happy and then feeding your answer back to you. What you probably don't know, however, is that our MOO scale is as accurate as the GARQ when it comes to separating happy from unhappy couples. That's because question 5 of our MOO scale is actually the same as question 31 of the official Dyadic Adjustment Scale (or GARQ). In a study published in the journal *Family Therapy*, Robin Goodwin reports that the answer to just that one single question on the Dyadic Adjustment Scale is as good at determining marital quality as the entire questionnaire combined. She calls this question "the magical question 31." Amazingly, it turns out that if you ask people how happy they are in their marriage, you can accurately discriminate happy, well-adjusted couples from unhappy, distressed couples. The best tool the experts have for figuring out how you're feeling is to ask you. So have faith in your own perceptions of your relationship. Experts can be helpful, but they don't have magical insights or a panacea for troubled marriages, so don't let them bamboozle you with big words or fancy quizzes. Trust that you and your spouse are the most experienced experts when it comes to your marriage, and that you are the world's *only* expert on what will make you personally happiest.

Too late to get help from the expert?

For centuries, we in Western culture have had a name for the first month of marriage. We call it "honeymoon" because it is the sweetest ("honey") of all possible months ("moons"). During this period, everything your spouse does or says makes you happier and more in love. Couples treat one another tenderly and bask in the passion they feel for one another.

There is, sadly, an analogy to this time in a marriage that is nearing its end. This time has no name and we don't acknowledge its characteristics, but it is just as clear how it affects attitudes and behaviors. We have come up with our own name for this period of time. We call this the "bittersun" period: "bitter" because we couldn't think of a better antonym for "honey," and "sun" because it lasts about a year, or one orbit around the sun.

The bittersun period starts when one (or both) spouse(s) loses the desire to stay married. Once you know in your heart that you no longer want to be married, the demise of your relationship is inevitable, but your mind may take some time to come to terms with that fact. The gap in time between what the heart knows and what the mind can accept is the bittersun period. During this time, everything your spouse does, no matter how innocuous, makes you less happy. One or both of you may still make efforts to preserve the marriage, but anger, betrayal and insecurity infect all of your interactions. Once the bittersun has begun, it may be too late to save the marriage, but a good deal of damage can be done by ending the marriage slowly. You and your spouse can take advantage of your close quarters to cause one another maximal pain, amplifying the resentment that you will carry with you into your divorce.

Often the first visit to a marriage counselor takes place during the early months of the bittersun. Unfortunately, a therapist can't save your marriage after your heart has quit any more than a doctor can save your life after your disease has become incurable. The difficulty is recognizing whether your heart has truly left your marriage and the bittersun has begun. A marriage counselor may be able to help you to examine your feelings, but you are the only person with knowledge of your own heart. It is up to you to be brutally honest with yourself and, if you have reached this point, begin the transition out of your marriage as gracefully as possible.

> There is a rhythm to the ending of a marriage just like the rhythm of a courtship—only backward. You try to start again but get into blaming over and over. Finally you are both worn out, exhausted, hopeless. Then lawyers are called in to pick clean the corpses. The death has occurred much earlier.
>
> —Erica Jong, *How To Save Your Own Life*

Conclusion

We hope that you are now better acquainted with the Expert Cow, and that you will be able to spot her tracks in self-help books and therapists' offices. We also hope that you don't let the Expert Cow sour your view of *all* marriage experts. Many marriage counselors are wise people who can provide insight and guidance during upsetting times. Just because there is no scientifically proven remedy for relationship problems does not mean that professional guidance has no value.

One of the best clues that a therapist or self-help book is operating as an Expert Cow is if you receive the message "You are a bad person if you won't continue your marriage." Maybe it's understandable for your religious leader or your spouse to throw that accusation at you (though we would hope that they wouldn't), but it is not an appropriate message from a therapist. The counseling community should not use its power over vulnerable individuals to create inappropriate pressure to preserve marriages. A good counselor will help to repair damaged relationships but will also help individuals to decide whether marriage is really their best path forward in life. The Expert Cow, on the other hand, is a blind advocate for the institution of marriage, and she will tell you anything to get you to do what she wants. To her, we say, "That's just 'grazy' talk."

References
1. Lebow, J.L., Chambers A.L., Christensen, A., Johnson, S.M. (2012). Research on the Treatment of Couple Distress. *Journal of Marital and Family Therapy*, 38(1),145–168.
2. Shadish, W.R., Baldwin, S.A. (2005). Effects of Behavioral Marital Therapy: A Meta-Analysis of Randomized Controlled Trials. *Journal of Consulting and Clinical Psychology*, 73(1), 6-14.
3. Hahlweg, K., Richter, D. (2010). Prevention of marital instability and distress: results of an 11-year longitudinal follow-up study. *Behaviour Research and Therapy*, 48, 377-383.
4. Heyman, R.E., Slep A.M.S. (2001). The Hazards of Predicting Divorce Without Crossvalidation. *Journal of Marriage and the Family*, 63(2), 473–479.

CHAPTER THREE
The Selfish Cow

> *All men seek happiness. This is without exception. The cause of some going to war, and of others avoiding it, is the same desire in both, attended with different views. The will never takes the least step but to this object. This is the motive of every action of every man, even of those who hang themselves.*
> —*Blaise Pascal*

Meet the Cow

The Selfish Cow is the most straightforward and the boldest of all of the Cows. She wants to tell you that staying married is unselfish and getting divorced is selfish. She shows up everywhere, sometimes hiding in plain sight (a neat trick for a gal who weighs 1000 pounds!). You will find her skulking behind comments your family and friends make, in popular media, even grazing in the back of your mind. You may not yet recognize her, but after you read this chapter you won't be able to stop noticing her all around you.

Caveat: Tipping over this Cow is not a defense of selfishness. It only involves recognizing that divorcing is not inherently a more selfish choice than staying married.

All generalizations are false

A common adjective applied to people choosing divorce is "selfish," as in: "You are selfish to break your vows to me just because you think that you can make a better life without me!" or, "You are selfish to pursue your own desires and happiness at the expense of your children."

According to Merriam-Webster's dictionary, selfish means "concerned excessively or exclusively with oneself : seeking or concentrating on one's own advantage, pleasure, or well-being without regard for others." This description matches the impression that many non-divorced people have about those who choose divorce: if these people cared about anyone other than themselves, they would suck it up and stay married.

Like all of the Sacred Cows, this attitude carries a kernel of truth that frequently breaks down when applied to specific situations and fails utterly when applied across the board. Or, as Mark Twain put it much more pithily, "All generalizations are false, including this one." Most of us can think of someone who remained in a loveless marriage for the sake of the children, thereby making a significant self-sacrifice. How we feel about that choice depends in large part on what we believe it cost the self-sacrificing spouse to stay and how much the children and other spouse gained (or lost) from that sacrifice.

Whether we realize it or not, most of us operate with some mix of religion-derived and utilitarian ethics. Religion-derived morality in this situation typically holds that it is bad to leave a marriage under any circumstance, no matter how happy or unhappy the situation makes everyone involved. To illustrate this, we have drawn a Selfishness Chart for a hypothetical unhappily married person we will call by the unisex name "Logan." Logan is considering leaving his/her marriage. We will graph his/her happiness on the x-axis and everyone else's happiness (e.g., spouse, children, in-laws, friends) on the y-axis. As you can see from our graph, Logan's happiness and everyone else's happiness is irrelevant to moral judgment from a typically religious point of view.

Selfishness Chart, Religious Perspective

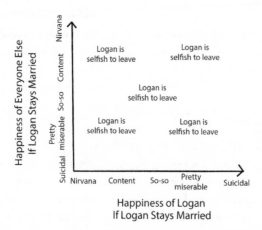

Now let's look at the same chart from a utilitarian perspective. Utilitarianism is a theory of ethics stating that the proper course of action is the one that maximizes overall happiness. In other words, the right thing to do is the thing that brings the most happiness to the most people. As you can see from the utilitarian perspective chart, at the extremes of happiness and unhappiness lie absurdity. In the middle lies a nuanced zone full of shades of gray, where the moral course of action is unclear.

Selfishness Chart, Utilitarian Perspective

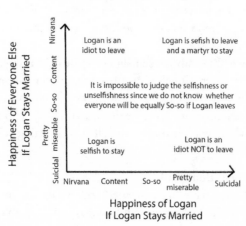

Most of us operate from some combination of these two charts. We are neither as judgmental as the first chart implies nor as purely logical as the second chart would indicate. Our knee-jerk reaction is to see people who choose divorce as selfish, but we can also be open to softening our judgment based upon the details of each case.

Who is selfish?

As noted above, the Merriam-Webster dictionary defines selfishness as concentrating on one's own happiness without regard to others. In real life though, when we call people selfish, we often mean that they do not put the happiness of others ahead of their own. Someone who decides to divorce is saying, "My happiness matters more than the happiness of my spouse and children." That does sound pretty selfish when you put it like that, doesn't it?

Some would say that we are all selfish in that our personal happiness is what we work hardest to maximize. When I give up a seat on the bus to an elderly person, I feel a rush of pleasure and improved sense of self-worth. When I refuse to give up my seat, my legs may feel less tired, but I am haunted by the unhappy knowledge that I did the wrong thing. What if I give up my seat because I'm trying to impress somebody else on the bus with my generous act? Or what if I give up my seat because a really stinky person sat down beside me and I'd rather not have to sit there anymore?

How we think about selfishness is heavily influenced by the details of each situation and the motivations of everyone involved. In order to explore the subject of selfishness in the context of divorce, we have devised a series of hypothetical situations where you must ask yourself who is acting selfishly.

Case 1. House Beautiful

Ayelet and Max have been married for twenty-six years. Max has been professionally successful, and Ayelet was able to stay home to raise their two children while enjoying a comfortable lifestyle. Max travels frequently, but he has been a good father and attentive husband. Despite this, Ayelet feels lonely. The children have left home, and she has not felt close to Max for many years. They have grown so far apart that Ayelet no longer even desires emotional or physical intimacy with Max. She had one brief extramarital affair when the children were young, and she is contemplating having another. Ayelet quit her marriage emotionally a long time ago and sometimes thinks about divorce, but she is too worried about losing their beautiful house with her beloved gardens as well as their close-knit community of friends.

Which of these statements is true?

A) Ayelet is a martyr for staying married to Max

B) Ayelet would be less selfish if she were to have a conversation with Max about how she feels, thereby risking losing her comfortable lifestyle

C) Max would definitely be happier if Ayelet said nothing to him and they continued as they are, with him living in blissful ignorance

D) Max would definitely be happier if Ayelet left him and he had the opportunity to find a new partner who actually loves him

If you answered B, then we agree with you. Ayelet is frightened by the possibility of divorce, and she is avoiding a conversation with Max for her own selfish motives. In theory, C or D might be correct also, since we don't know what would make Max happiest.

Case 2. No Exit

Bob has been married to Sally for twenty-five years, but Bob is no longer happy being married to Sally. Bob can still appreciate Sally's better qualities, but he no longer enjoys being around her. They have gone to marriage counselors on and off for years, but this has not made Bob any happier, and he is now considering divorce. Sally reminds Bob that she gave up other suitors to marry him, and she has planned her whole life around him. She tells him that she is too old to start her life over, and he has no right to ditch her just because he isn't happy. Sally implies that if Bob isn't willing to stick with the promise he made twenty-five years ago, then Bob is a selfish, worthless good-for-nothing.

Which of these statements is true?
A) Sally is a talented manipulator, and she should consider a future in politics
B) Bob should point out to Sally that if she really loved him, she would care about his happiness
C) Sally is being selfish for refusing to even consider putting Bob's happiness ahead of her own
D) All of the above

Yes, we picked D too, although we had some reservations about Sally's future political career, to be honest. (She was laying it on a bit thick, don't you think?) We agree that Sally is selfish to demand that Bob sacrifice his happiness for her sake when she seems unwilling to consider doing the same for him. Bob is being selfish by considering divorce, because leaving would entail putting his happiness ahead of Sally's. However, Sally is also selfish to try to keep Bob married to her when she knows that is not what he wants.

Case 3. Holier Than Thou
Malcolm is a minister of an evangelical church; his wife Chanelle helped him to start the church, and she still functions as the chief operating officer, keeping everything running smoothly. Malcolm and Chanelle are good companions and colleagues, but they now sleep in separate bedrooms. Malcolm told his wife that it was her snoring keeping him awake at night, but in reality, he can't stand sharing physical intimacy with her. Malcolm has admitted to himself that he is gay, and he abhors that part of himself. He has never sought out a gay partner, but Malcolm secretly indulges in gay pornography while his wife is asleep, and

he has begun flirting online. He feels guilty, and he is terrified of being found out. If Chanelle discovered his secret, he would risk losing his living, his church, his community and his marriage.

Which of these statements is true?

A) Malcolm is putting his own interests ahead of Chanelle's by not telling her the truth

B) All of the above

That one was a freebie.

Case 4. War of the Roses

Angela and Pierre hate one another. They have three teenaged daughters who have been watching their hostilities for years. Every night at dinner, the parents trade condescending remarks via their children. Pierre has openly had affairs, and Angela has tried to use this fact to get her daughters to take her side in the ongoing marital war. If you asked Angela and Pierre why they are still married, they would say that they are not the sort of people who divorce, and they need to stay together for the sake of their children.

Which of the following statements is true?

A) Angela and Pierre are both making the ultimate self-sacrifice for their children

B) Everyone (including the children) would have been better off if Angela and Pierre had divorced long ago

C) Angela and Pierre would be less selfish if they sought professional help for themselves and their children and if they at least considered divorce

D) Wasn't there a movie called *The War of the Roses*?

We agree that any of these could be true. Angela and Pierre are suffering, and their children are suffering too. It isn't clear to us what the least selfish course of action would be vis-à-vis marriage and divorce, but it is clear that Angela and Pierre could do better by one another (and by their children) by making some different choices.

Case 5. Baby Blues

Ivan and Soledad have had a mostly happy marriage, but since the birth of their first child, Soledad has become unhappy. She feels that Ivan does not do enough to help her around the house, and she is jealous of his career. She is glad that Ivan is able to support her financially, but she is also bitter that he gets to have all of the fun, reward and recognition for his work while she is home straining fresh applesauce. Ivan encourages her to start looking for work that she might find fulfilling, and he hires help for her at home. But the more unhappy Soledad becomes, the more demanding and angry she becomes with Ivan. Finally, Ivan threatens to divorce her if she will not agree to work with him to get back to a happier marriage.

Udderly Personal

Sometimes, leaving a long-term relationship is the only way for two people to grow. Six years into my marriage, I woke up one morning and didn't recognize my life. I was not where I thought I would be, and the external trappings of my life, including the way I was relating to my husband, in no way matched my interior landscape. I didn't want to jettison the relationship, having invested so much, but every time I made a move to be more personally authentic, we would start fighting. The conversation would always begin with his accusation: "You've changed! You are not the same person I chose to be with!" This was quickly followed by further accusations that I was selfishly thinking only of myself and my own needs. I would try to justify myself, but inside I was thinking, "Well, duh! Who doesn't change? And isn't understanding, communicating and acting on your needs essential to living an honest life?" A well-functioning relationship should involve real efforts to accommodate and facilitate both changes in circumstance and changes in each other. Otherwise, what you are left with is nothing more than a quick-drying, concrete monument to past love. When I finally realized that that is what we were busy creating together, that we were both truly holding each other back, that's when I knew that the relationship had to end.

—Moving on in Montpelier

Which of the following statements are true?

A) It's not really clear whether anyone is being particularly selfish here or not

B) This quiz is getting old and I'm ready to move on

C) What's for lunch?

D) All of the above

Okay, we will stop now. You get the point. What seems selfish or selfless to us depends greatly on the circumstances, and it would be wrong to assume that everyone who considers divorce is being selfish and that everyone who chooses to stay married is doing so for the purest, most selfless reasons. As you can see from our examples, there are situations where it is more selfish to stay in a marriage than to end it, and there are many circumstances where it just isn't obvious what the most selfish course of action would be. We hope that this is the first step in tipping the Selfish Cow: the acknowledgement that "selfish" is probably not a valid generalization to make about divorce, and that we should understand the whole story before we leap to judgment.

Put on your own oxygen mask first

Before leaving the tarmac, passengers are instructed by the airplane crew to "put on your oxygen mask before assisting anyone else." We have to listen to this every single time we get on a plane because most people will put the safety of their loved ones ahead of their own safety. Humans are wired to sacrifice themselves for their families. The Federal Aviation Administration understands the danger of this instinct, because in the case of a depressurized cabin, nobody can be of use to his or her loved ones after losing consciousness.

Many marriage self-help books acknowledge that this danger occurs in marriage as well, in the sense that people who allow themselves to drown in unhappiness will drag their spouses and children into misery with them. The self-help mantra is that you must take responsibility for your own happiness and let your spouse do the same for him or herself. Strangely, the notion that "taking care of your own happiness" while leaving others to fend for themselves bears more than a passing resemblance to "selfishness" doesn't come up. Maybe that's because these books only suggest that you take responsibility for your happiness *within* your marriage, but they don't consider that you might follow your happiness all the way *out* of your marriage. It seems that if you stand up for yourself and can get your spouse to give you what you think you need, then you are being brave. But if your spouse can't give you what you need, and you decide to leave your marriage, then you are being selfish. Moooo.

Avoidance of pain as a substitute for happiness

If Blaise Pascal was right, and the fundamental aim of every human act is to increase personal happiness, then why do so many people stay in bad marriages? We don't claim to have the whole answer, because every relationship and personality is unique. We propose, however, that Sigmund Freud had a partial answer for this. Freud stated that human beings strive for happiness, and that this endeavor has two sides: a positive and a negative aim. The positive aim speaks for itself; this is what we think of when we imagine "striving for happiness." Importantly, the negative aim is the avoidance of pain or displeasure, and this may be as powerful a motivator as pleasure seeking.

It is probable that many people consider leaving a bad marriage to seek greater happiness in what Freud would call the "positive" aim but end up staying because of the "negative" aim, or avoidance of pain. In other words, when they consciously or subconsciously do the calculus, they decide that the possible benefit of finding greater happiness outside of a dysfunctional marriage is not worth suffering the pain associated with leaving a familiar situation. Often the low-grade, persistent ache of staying in a bad relationship is easier to manage on any given day than the brief but highly concentrated awfulness of leaving.

We cannot second-guess the wisdom of such choices without knowing every detail of the circumstances. Accordingly, we are not saying that such a calculation is wrong. We would venture to guess, however, that people who make this choice are particularly vulnerable to the Selfish Sacred Cow. The vulnerability works like this: "I am not happy in my marriage, but I am not leaving. The reason I'm not leaving is mostly because I think that the pain of leaving will outweigh the pain of staying. That doesn't sound like a great choice when I phrase it like that, though. I would rather tell myself that I am staying because it is the noble and unselfish thing for me to do. If that is true, then people who make a different choice (to seek a divorce) are acting selfishly. Q.E.D."

It is from this type of logic that Sacred Cows are born. Once we are sensitized to the Sacred Cows, however, we can teach ourselves and others to correct the logic and send the herd of Sacred Cows back to the barn.

The hard work of marriage

Our society has some code phrases for "you are selfish to get divorced," and one of these is "marriage is hard work." The implication is that the person choosing divorce is too weak or selfish to do the hard work of marriage. This message is often delivered with a dollop of self-satisfaction on the part of a messenger who believes him or herself to be the Hercules of marital labor. This concept that marriage is (and should be) hard work has permeated our entire culture, like the tribal knowledge that *Here Comes Honey Boo Boo* is the worst television show ever created. In fact, we dare you to say at your next social gathering, "I think that marriage is a total cakewalk," (or for that matter, that creation of *Honey Boo Boo* was a brilliant stroke of genius) so that you can see the appalled expressions on everyone's faces. Yet strangely, although everyone agrees that marriage is a constant slog and reality TV is abysmal, people continue to get married in droves and *Honey Boo Boo* draws millions of viewers.

Could there be another Sacred Cow hiding here?

Before we examine the hard work of marriage a little more closely, let us step back for a moment and consider the position of someone on the brink of ending his or her marriage. Setting aside the question of whether it is selfish to end a marriage, let's look at what is hard and what is brave. A person leaving a marriage risks being on the receiving end of anger, coldness and censure from family and friends. He or she risks losing time with children and having to live with the guilt of destroying a nuclear family. Some people may be rejected by their churches and communities. There are risks of financial insecurity and the uncertainty of starting life over again as a single person. On top of this, most people know ahead of time that they are going to have to suffer through this process without help from some of the very people from whom they are most used to receiving support during hard times. Anyone willing to go through such a process is clearly doing something hard and being brave (again, leaving aside whether it is a laudable choice). Now, imagine that this person is being advised that staying married is *even* harder and requires *even more* fortitude and bravery than divorce. What horrors do you think the advisor predicts that marriage has in store for this poor soul?

Obviously, "hard work" can't be the whole story, because if it were, nobody would get married. One of the following must therefore be true: A) The benefits of marriage outweigh the hard work; B) Not being married is its own form of even harder work; or C) We are all a bunch of workaholics.

Any of these options might be true, but most people will probably agree with A (the benefits of marriage outweigh the hard work). We work hard at a lot of things in life because we believe that our hard work will pay some kind of dividend. When a mountaineer is slogging up Mount Everest and losing extremities to frostbite, that is very hard work. The mountaineer is not a masochist though, but rather judges the reward of summiting to be worth the price of the suffering. Similarly, when people put hard work into marriage, they are not usually driven by masochism or a moral imperative to be industrious; they are expecting (or hoping for) the reward of a happy relationship. In this way, the hard work of marriage is probably better compared to the effort required to maintain friendship than the effort of mountain climbing. Marital satisfaction derives much more from companionship than from the pride of weathering hardships at the limit of human endurance. Nobody gets a trophy for surviving a bad marriage.

If the purpose of hard work is to maintain or regain a happy marriage, then instead of throwing an arm over a troubled friend's shoulder and saying, "Buddy, marriage is hard work," a concerned friend should probably enumerate the benefits of marriage that make the hard work worthwhile. We're not talking about a further guilt trip, like "Kids are happier when their parents are married," but the real palpable benefits that make us *want* to be married even when the going gets rough. These are benefits like affection, nurturing, attention, yummy food, devotion, companionship, clean clothes, social validation, compassion, economic rewards, surprise birthday parties, prestige, security, parenting help, fun, intimacy, sex, someone to walk the dog, emotional support, a warm bed and lots of love (to name a few). Yet when the Selfish Cow rings the doorbell, she is seldom there to extoll the virtues of marriage. Instead, she is coming to extoll the virtues of hard work. Let's hear this directly from the Cow's mouth, as our Selfish Cow has graciously agreed to a brief interview:

> **Author:** "Good day, Ms. Selfish Cow. Thank you for agreeing to our invitation for an interview."
>
> **Selfish Cow:** "Why, thank moo for inviting me!"
>
> **Author:** "We have heard you allude to the virtues of the hard work of marriage. Would you care to elaborate for our audience?"
>
> **Selfish Cow:** "Oh yes. People who leave their marriages because they are unwilling to do the hard work required to make their marriages great are lazy good-for-nothings."
>
> **Author:** "Ms. Cow, how can you tell when lack of hard

work is the reason for marital unhappiness?"

Selfish Cow: "That's easy! I can tell because the marriage is unhappy. If the couple were working hard, the marriage would be happy!"

Author: "It sounds like you believe that every marriage can be made great through sufficient application of hard work."

Selfish Cow: "Well, dearie, the difference between try and triumph is a little umph!"

Author: "Let's say things are going very badly for a couple despite a great deal of effort on their part. How long would you advise these people to keep working at improving their marriage?"

Selfish Cow: "Why, until they make the marriage happy again, of course!"

Author: "I see. This seems like a circular argument."

Selfish Cow: "What's wrong with that? Cows love to make circles! Well, I must hoof it out of here … Bye!"

As the Selfish Cow herself makes clear, she believes that every marriage can be made fulfilling if both parties just keep their noses to the nuptial grindstone. The Selfish Cow does not acknowledge that equal rewards are not found in every marriage, and she seems to think that hard work alone is what makes people virtuous. We're not sure that this is the whole story, though, so let's see if we can get her to answer another question:

Author: "Ms. Selfish Cow, Ms. Selfish Cow, just another moment of your time, please!"

Selfish Cow: "Quit your prodding! All right. Go ahead."

Author: "What if my best friend from childhood had grown up to be self-centered, and she took advantage of me consistently without giving anything back. Would you tell me that I needed to work harder to keep her as my best friend?"

Selfish Cow: "Don't be silly. Of course not!"

Author: "Thank you, Ms. Cow! See you back at the ranch!"

As you can see from her answer, what the Selfish Cow cares about most is not the hard work itself, but maintaining the marriage. Like all of the Sacred Cows, she is using the tools at her disposal to make people feel bad about divorce. She promotes hard work as a virtue because she knows that nobody wants to think about him or herself as lazy. She doesn't expect martyrdom in other areas of life, however. She recognizes that some rewards are not worth the effort, and that some rewards are unattainable through hard work. Nevertheless, when it comes to marriage, she believes that every relationship is worth an infinite amount of effort and that the effort should continue even when it cannot cause a square peg to fit into a round hole.

Udderly Personal

I have never understood why everyone thinks that marriage is such hard work. Between the sporadic downs, ours has been pretty effortless, as I think a good marriage should be. We fight sometimes, and we don't always make each other perfectly happy, but mostly we just like being together. Our burdens are lighter because we share them, and our happiness is more intense because we share that also. I don't see how being married can be more work than being single, and if it is harder, I don't see the point of staying married. That's not to say that you shouldn't try to work through the rough patches, but the rewards of marriage should be accruing in the present or at least in the near future, not in heaven for a painful life rightly lived.
—Puzzled in Peoria

Defining the hard work of marriage

One question the Selfish Cow tries to avoid answering is "What *is* the hard work of marriage?" Although the phrase "hard work of marriage" permeates our culture, we don't often stop to wonder what it means. To bring marital toil into better focus, we trolled marriage self-help books and online sources for statements about the hard work of marriage, and we asked our friends and family as well. We have distilled the answers we received into the following six categories:

1. Marriage requires that we experience and resolve conflicts.
2. Marriage requires compromise.
3. Marriage requires that we treat our spouse nicely.
4. Marriage requires conscious effort to keep romance alive.
5. Life throws a lot of curveballs at married couples.
6. Marriage is hard work because you're not allowed to leave when you feel like it.

It is worth taking a few moments to think through the ways in which these types of hard work feature in marriage. We will begin by examining the first three points about conflict resolution, compromise, and kindness since these ideas are interrelated.

There is no question that conflict is stressful and that successful marriages require give-and-take as well as kindness. This is true of virtually all human relationships, and the requirement for compromise, conflict management and kindness increases with the intimacy and significance of the relationship. When your friend Andy is rude to the barista at Starbucks, he may only suffer from a little slower service, whereas when Andy is rude to his husband, the fallout can ruin his whole day.

Imagine that your friend Andy tells you that he is unhappy in his marriage. He and his husband Jake fight constantly, and Andy has begun to dread going home in the evening. If you know that Andy is a temperamental guy without great talent for diplomacy, you might advise him to see a marriage counselor or maybe read a good book about managing conflict. You might remind him that Jake's needs are just as important as his own, and that compassion and kindness can smooth over a lot of raw feelings. If Andy takes your advice, then perhaps his marriage will improve. If Andy doesn't take your advice, you might be legitimately concerned that this marriage (as well as any potential future marriage Andy might enter into) will not last, since he is not working on the skills required to live happily in close quarters with another human being.

Now imagine that Andy is a super sweet guy who tries

to give Jake everything he wants. Jake never seems to want to give anything back, however. For a decade, Andy has tried to make Jake happy only to be rewarded with coldness, disdain and more demands. Are you going to advise Andy to work harder at compromising and being kind? Probably not, since effort without reward is not best described as "hard work" but rather "masochism."

Finally, imagine a third situation where Andy and Jake get along fine. They agree about everything, and they are the envy of their friends because they seem like the perfect couple. Andy tells you that they never have sex anymore and they haven't shared real intimacy in years. They have worked with three different therapists and have tried many exercises to rekindle their passion, but they haven't been able to identify any problems or find a solution. Now Jake has told Andy that he wants out of the marriage. It's hard to imagine how Andy could achieve a happy marriage under these circumstances by working harder at resolving conflicts, compromising, or being kind. Yet because "hard work of marriage" is usually bandied about as a vague and nebulous concept, it's likely that somebody (not you, of course) is going to tell Andy (or Jake) that more hard work is the key to a solution.

These three scenarios illustrate that some marital problems can be solved (or at least improved) by skillful conflict management, compromise, and kindness. Other marital problems are entirely orthogonal, having nothing to do with lack of compromise or kindness. Still other marital problems are created by unilateral compromises, proving that not all marriages involving compromise are good marriages. In business there is a wise saying that sometimes the best deal to do is no deal at all. Marriage can occasionally be like that too.

Another frequently cited aspect of the "hard work of marriage" is the effort required to fan the flames of romance. Presumably, it is creating time for romance that is hard work, because lighting candles or sharing a nice dinner should not require a lot of elbow grease. Carving time out of a busy schedule for date night can be challenging, but the reward is an enjoyable evening. (If an evening alone with your spouse feels like a recreational root canal, then it is worth at least considering whether you are married to the right person.)

Beyond the common challenge of scheduling couple time and the (hopefully) rare challenge of enduring a painful night with one's spouse without the distraction of television, there lurks a darker, more complex reason that romance creation is considered hard work. Heady romantic feelings are hard to achieve, if "achieve" is even the correct word. Candles, lingerie and quiet dinners create a fertile environment for romantic feelings to flourish, but the feelings themselves cannot be willed into being. Romantic feelings arise from a mysterious chemistry of love, admiration and desire, and while they can be squelched by stress and neglect, they cannot be created by relaxation and attention.

The elusive nature of romantic feelings can make date night feel like a failure. If a romantic evening is routinely followed by crankiness about having to make school lunches and a cold shoulder in bed, the couple may feel that they are not getting romance right, and that more effort must be required. Nobody has invented the magic formula to amplify romantic feelings, however, let alone recreate feelings that no longer exist. If carving out couple time to do things you enjoy together is never associated with romantic feelings, then rather than feeling guilty about not being up to the hard work of marriage, you should perhaps be asking yourself whether you are trying to shut the barn door after the cows have gone.

Sometimes when people talk about the hard work of marriage, they refer to external forces that can put stress on a marriage, such as job loss or illness. Life does throw a lot of curveballs at married couples, but it is not fair to blame most of these misfortunes on marriage. Unemployment and illness are no easier for single people to bear than for married people, and divorce doesn't generally reduce the number of misfortunes that fate throws at people. Unless one's spouse is a curveball magnet, curveballs come to find all of us at about the same rate regardless of marital status.

Finally, some people consider marriage to be hard work because you're not allowed to leave when you feel like it. Apart from the fact that lots of people do leave their marriages, this represents circular reasoning. It is like saying, "The Pope is infallible; therefore, what he just said is true." Or, more to the point, "Commitments are hard because you have to stick with them." This may be a true statement, but it is completely uninformative.

The hardworking Selfish Cow

We are not arguing that marriage does not at times require hard work. Every relationship, perhaps every human endeavor worth undertaking, sometimes requires hard work. When the Selfish Cow accuses unhappy couples of not working hard enough, however, she is trying to shift attention away from unsolvable problems and put the blame on "lazy spouses." This has two effects that are pleasing to the Selfish Cow: First, it means that there is no excuse for anyone to divorce, since she is proposing that harder work can fix all problems. Second, it causes people to see themselves as failures when their marriages end, creating extra incentive not to "give up" on an unhappy marriage.

In the larger picture, the Selfish Cow is saying that people who get divorced are not just lazy, they are fundamentally more selfish than people who stay married. As we showed at the beginning of the chapter, there are selfish reasons to stay married as well as selfish reasons to get divorced. The Selfish Cow will never be convinced that divorced people are as good as married people, but let's leave her with one last question at the conclusion of this chapter: Who does she think benefits from people selflessly staying in unhappy marriages?

Selfish Cow: "Moo, that's easy. Everyone of course!"
Author: "Presumably the person selflessly staying isn't benefitting, or it wouldn't be a selfless act, would it?"
Selfish Cow: "Well, the other spouse and children will benefit!"

Author: "Do you really think that most people would be happy being married to someone who would rather leave? Or that children benefit from growing up with one or both parents feeling miserable?"

Selfish Cow: "Moo, people don't *stay* unhappy if they do the hard work of marriage. Pretty soon they will be happy again!"

Author: "But then we are back where we started: It is not a selfless act to stay if everyone ends up happy."

Selfish Cow: "Moo!! You are trying to trick me. You are going in circles!"

Author: "Ms. Cow, I do believe that it is you who is chasing your tail."

Udderly Personal

When I was a teenage girl in the 1970s, I had the same stupid poster on my wall as most of my friends. You remember, it went like this:

"If you love something set it free.
If it comes back to you it's yours.
If not, it was never meant to be."

How was I ever to guess that this was going to apply to my ex-husband? I was so angry when he told me that he wanted a divorce. I thought that he was wrong, a selfish pig to be honest. But when he said to me, "If you really care about me, then you will not try to keep me in a cage," I remembered the poster. It's funny how ideas come back around to bite you in the butt, isn't it?

—Irritated in Idaho

CHAPTER FOUR
The Defective Cow

Scientists have discovered a food that diminishes a woman's sex drive by 90%. It's called a wedding cake.
—*Anonymous*

Meet the Cow

The Defective Cow is a master of disguise. Though she takes many forms, she always uses fear and shame as her tools for keeping people in line. This Cow looks for an opening to make you feel that you are the problem to be fixed. She wants you to know that only defective people are unhappy in their marriages, and your defectiveness will be plain to everyone if you divorce. The Defective Cow loves to quote experts about how sad you will be if you don't listen to her and how happy you must be to be married.

Caveat: Tipping over this Cow removes unproductive fear and shame surrounding the decision about whether to divorce, but it does not excuse bad behavior. Society has no right to tell you that you are defective for being unhappily married, but surely we all have some behaviors that could use some work.

Marriage and lost libido

It is a pervasive stereotype in our culture that women lose interest in sex after marriage. Our society acknowledges that waning desire may be a problem for married men also, but women are generally considered to be the rate-limiting factor in the bedroom. Many explanations for the disappearance of women's interest in sex have been proposed, including fatigue, stress, hormonal shifts, poor body image and low self-esteem. The implication is that there is something wrong with either the wife or her lifestyle, and fixing this problem can restore lost desire. This could very well be true, but there are also other reasons that perfectly normal, well-adjusted and non-sleep-deprived women lose interest in having sex with their husbands, and these reasons we don't hear so much about.

One reason for lost libido that you seldom hear is, "She's just not that into him." You would think that this reason would come up more, because it's a common phenomenon in non-marital romantic relationships. When a boyfriend or girlfriend no longer seems desirable, there is rarely a necessity for excuses about hormones or fatigue; everyone accepts that you can be "into" someone for a while and then "not-so-into" that person later on. Some married couples must lose interest in the same way that boyfriends and girlfriends lose interest, but we as a society do not acknowledge the "not-that-into-him/her" phenomenon when it comes to marriage. We avoid it because if we acknowledge that a married woman (we'll call her Barbara) is normal and healthy but not attracted to her husband William, then we're stuck either pushing her to have sex she doesn't want (not a choice that our society can admit to making) or advising her to get out of her marriage (also something our culture can't get behind). Ergo, says our cultural psyche, if I can't live with the implications of Barbara not being into William, then it must be the case that Barbara *is* into William but she has some other problem. There, now don't we all feel better?

The Barbaras of the world can end up feeling defective, because appointments with psychologists, gynecologists and endocrinologists can't usually fix her "problem." While William can take a little blue pill to help pique his interest, no equivalent pill exists (yet) for Barbara. Even if Barbara could take a Viagra pill equivalent, this would presumably help only the physical aspect of arousal without addressing emotional and mental aspects. What the Barbaras (and some of the Williams) of the world need is a road map for how to become attracted to their marriage partners again, and such a road map does not exist.

You now may be thinking, "That's not true that those road maps don't exist! A whole industry exists to help people create more intimacy in marriage." You are right; intimacy creation is big business in this country. Offering to help to create intimacy sidesteps the point, however, that some people no longer crave intimacy with their spouses. It also misses the point that intimacy is not the same as love, and that neither love nor intimacy is perfectly correlated with desire. Further, in analogy to the weight-loss industry, the large number of relationship self-help books and seminars available to consumers may be an indication of the scope of the problem, not evidence that good solutions exist.

$$Love \neq DESIRE$$

$$Intimacy \neq DESIRE$$

$$Love + Intimacy + ? = DESIRE$$

figure this out ↑ and you will be rich!!!

Simplified Equation

$$\cancel{Love} + \cancel{Intimacy} + ? = DESIRE$$

not strictly required

$$\therefore \ ? = DESIRE$$

The Defective Cow is a huge fan of the intimacy creation industry, because it gives her something positive to hide behind.

She categorically rejects the notion that married people could simply lose interest in one another romantically and sexually, and she cites books and marriage gurus to prove that she is right. If the Defective Cow cannot convince Barbara that her problem is hormonal or psychological, then she will work on the angle that Barbara's problem is a bad attitude. If Barbara can just bring herself to ask William to alter his sexual routines, or if she can face her own fears, or if she can share her most cherished aspirations with William, or do whatever the book or guru is prescribing, then all will be well. If all is still not well, then that just proves that Barbara is defective, because passion is guaranteed to those who follow the instructions properly.

"Your problem is that you want the wrong kind of marriage"

Lori Gottlieb writes in her book *Marry Him: The Case for Settling for Mr. Good Enough* that "According to my married friends, once you're married, it's not so much about whom you want to go on a tropical vacation with; it's about whom you want to run a household with. Marriage isn't a constant passion-fest; it's more like a partnership formed to run a very small, mundane nonprofit business." She goes on to say, "Having a solid, like-minded teammate in life is pleasurable in its own way, and for most people, it's certainly better than not having one at all."

This rational if unromantic view of marriage rings true for many couples. It also makes perfect sense that people living in such business arrangements have less than ideal sex lives. If Barbara is married to William because he is a solid citizen, a good wage earner and a reliable partner in their mundane nonprofit, then she may have what she wants in marriage. Is there any reason she should want to have sex with William, though? We can all think of friends we respect and even love, but who do not interest us in the least sexually. If Barbara married William because she wanted a business partner, then a passionate sexual relationship would be nice, but it certainly shouldn't be expected.

When we asked Lori Gottlieb how she sees individuals reconciling a business attitude towards marriage with the expectation of a good sex life, she pointed out that most people are thinking about marriage in the opposite way when they tie the knot. "Most people begin marriage with deep expectations of romantic love and passion," she said, "but they forget about the business aspect." This perspective is supported by the research of anthropologist Helen Fisher, who reports that 91% of American women and 86% of American men say they would not marry someone unless they were in love with him or her, even if this person had every single trait they were looking for in a spouse.

Gottlieb went on to tell us that high levels of passion and desire in romantic relationships last only for about the first eighteen months, a phase that corresponds with the "dopamine-flooded brain." It is therefore not realistic to expect a continuing high level of desire over time. Interestingly, although advancing age is often blamed for waning desire, Gottlieb informed us that a much stronger predictor for the death of libido is how long couples have been together monogamously. Women lose interest in monogamous relationships more quickly than do men, and at a certain point, the only thing for a person like Barbara to do, according to Gottlieb, is "to get a new partner, which she doesn't want to do, because she wants to be in the marriage."

If Lori Gottlieb is correct, then the Defective Cow may be taking the wrong tack. The Defective Cow should not be suggesting that Barbara visit psychologists and endocrinologists; she should instead say to Barbara, "Look, hon, nobody wants to have sex after twenty years of marriage. Get real. You could find a new guy and rediscover your libido, but pretty soon you'll get tired of the new guy too. So just remember what a great partner William has been and give up on the sex thing already."

That sounds awfully depressing for all of the married people out there. If monogamy is the natural enemy of desire, then is there any hope for long-term passion in marriage? If Barbara left William, would she have any chance of finding someone who would continue to appeal to her sexually over the years? Helen Fisher, an expert on sex, love and marriage, gives us a resounding "maybe." Fisher and colleagues studied people who claimed to be still wild about their longtime spouse after an average of twenty-one years of marriage. Participants were asked to look at a photograph of their sweetheart while undergoing a brain scan. The researchers found that the brains of these middle-aged men and women showed much the same activity as those of young lovers who had been intensely in love for an average of only seven months.

This research suggests that head-over-heels love and attraction lasts long term for a minority of couples. So divorced Barbara *could* find a new spouse who would still make her swoon after twenty years of marriage, but she sure as heck shouldn't count on it. Barbara may also still have great affection for William, and she may highly value his companionship, even if the idea of canoodling with William is unappealing to her. Barbara's best shot at happiness may therefore be to settle into a sexless but companionable relationship with William. We don't want to tell the Defective Cow how to do her job, but shouldn't she stop telling Barbara that she is defective and become the "Nobody-is-having-sex-so-get-used-to-it" Cow?

Not really. The Defective Cow persists because sexless marriages are often unstable. It turns out that people really do want to canoodle with *someone*. If married couples were to just admit that there was going to be no more smooching and no more sex in their relationships, then the chance that one or both of them will look for intimacy elsewhere is high. The Defective Cow is therefore motivated to convince both Barbara and William that it is abnormal for Barbara not to want to have sex with William, and that by using the correct techniques, Barbara's "problem" can be fixed.

The magic passion pill

Barbara wants to desire William again so that they can become happier, and she is open to the Defective Cow's suggestion to try new techniques. Quite possibly, some of the fixes proposed by the self-help industry could rekindle Barbara's passion, although the large number of self-help books and marriage counselors in this country indicate that nobody has nailed the magic formula for creating passionate marriages. (If somebody did discover the magic formula, then everyone *else* would stop writing books on the subject, including us.)

Let us take a brief tour of some of the common solutions offered for creation of greater passion and ask ourselves why none of them represents the magic pill that we wish we could give to Barbara:

Empathetic listening and sharing. Many experts encourage the sharing of feelings, goals, dreams, and desires to recreate the intimacy of new relationships. When people first fall in love, they crave to know and to be known. The smallest details about cereal preferences or favorite colors seem fascinating, and new lovers spend hours talking about things as lofty as their most cherished desires and as mundane as their sixth-grade science project. Once a couple has been together for a long time, this kind of sharing generally drops off precipitously. This is not only because all of the favorite cereals and colors become known, but also because the demands of the rest of the world push out opportunities for romance.

If Barbara and William have stopped sharing or listening to one another because they have been distracted, then a program designed to get them talking again might help. There are two reasons why this does not represent a magic passion pill for Barbara, however. First, intimacy does not necessarily lead to passion. Barbara can feel as intimate with William as she does with her closest friends while having no more sexual desire for her husband than she has for her friends. (Some experts, such as psychotherapist Esther Perel, believe that intimacy actually stifles desire. If this is true, then intimacy creation could actually be counterproductive for Barbara and William.)

Second, Barbara and William may have stopped listening

to one another because they no longer crave knowledge of one another. If Barbara is not in love with William, she may not care to hear about the details of his trip to the dentist or his frustration with his lack of career direction. Barbara can listen to what William has to say, parrot it back and validate his perspective, but that won't make her feel closer to him if Barbara fundamentally finds William uninteresting.

Add a little romance. A common suggestion for recovering passion (or perhaps finding it for the first time) is to ratchet up the romance. Go out for a candlelit dinner, buy new lingerie, visit a favorite old haunt from your courtship days. Some experts suggest reliving happy memories together, like the wedding day or first encounter. These all seem like good ideas. In fact, they are such good ideas that Barbara and William have probably already tried many of them. If they needed a self-help book to tell them to go on dates together, and if going on some dates inspired them to have hot sex, then there was probably never much wrong with their relationship to begin with (other than surprising lack of social intuition). On the other hand, if Barbara and William are no longer into one another, flowers and candles sadly do not represent a magic passion pill. If they did, there would be a florist shop on every street corner instead of a Starbucks.

Fake it till you make it. We have all heard a lot about the power of positive thinking, and this plays a big part in marriage advice as well. A number of exercises designed to improve intimacy and rekindle passion involve thinking or saying nice things about one's partner every day. Such an exercise might help Barbara if she knows William to be a wonderful, admirable person, but she has simply lost sight of his better qualities in the daily grind of life. It could also work if Barbara is a highly suggestible person, but in that case, feelings of intimacy and/or passion would be unlikely to stick if Barbara does not actually think highly of William. Analogously, you may have rushed out to buy a new vacuum cleaner because of a convincing advertisement, but once you brought the vacuum home, no amount of reminding yourself about what they said in the ad would make you enthusiastic about the vacuum if it just didn't get the carpet clean.

Forget about intimacy, stand up for yourself. One popular marriage guru, David Schnarch, author of *Passionate Marriage*, takes a radical approach to intimacy. He states that the whole concept of intimacy involving reciprocity is wrong. He has created the term "self-validated intimacy" to refer to his idea that as long as you have a strong sense of yourself, you can experience intimacy even if your partner is deeply contemplating the car's need for an oil change while you're revealing your most cherished dreams and desires. Over time, it can apparently get easier to self-disclose and feel intimate with a partner who has neutral or even negative responses. If intimacy does not in fact require spousal involvement, Barbara might as well replace William with a potted rubber plant. That way she would not have to listen to complaints about her waning libido.

The bottom line for Barbara is that if she is still fundamentally into William, then it is worth her while to try to uncover her latent desire using whatever techniques she can. Although none of the above methods represents some kind of guaranteed fix, there is little downside to trying. On the other hand, if Barbara is no longer into William—if she has fallen out of love with him and no longer finds him romantically or sexually appealing—then she should not listen to the Defective Cow telling her that there is something wrong with her. The Defective Cow wants Barbara to believe that the reason empathetic listening, date night, positive thinking and "self-validated intimacy" have not yet fixed her marriage is because Barbara is not doing it right. She tells Barbara that there is no reason she can't have the marriage she wants to have with William other than the fact that Barbara is defective and unenlightened. We say that's a load of Sacred Cow poop.

Realistic expectations

We briefly discussed a good reason why the Defective Cow might not want married couples to simply resign themselves to a passionless relationship. Once a person realizes that his/her spouse will never be more than a friend or roommate, then that person has to be honest with him/herself about realistic choices: a life of celibacy, extramarital relationships or divorce. This causes instability in the marriage and sometimes the outcome the Defective Cow is trying hardest to avoid. Since the Defective Cow wants everyone to stay married, and since she sees that marriages can become loveless and passionless, she knows that she needs a backup strategy. For those who are giving up hope about rediscovering passion in marriage, she turns to experts who can make resignation seem noble.

If Barbara and William got married with the expectation that marriage would make them happy, then they presumably weigh the parts of their marriage that continue to bring happiness against the parts that don't, and they would at least consider ending their marriage if unhappiness predominated. On the other hand, if they married with an expectation that their own personal happiness would take a backseat to economic security and social stability for themselves and their children, they probably wouldn't get so worked up about the lack of passion in their marriage.

The Defective Cow wants more of the second scenario, and so she sides with conservative marriage experts who mourn the loss of old-fashioned values. In the 1950s and earlier, these divorce experts say, people married to raise a family, or to be economically secure, or to have a nice home and yard. Beginning in the 1960s, cultural norms shifted towards marrying for love. David Popenoe, sociologist and founder of the National Marriage Project, wrote, "Traditionally, marriage has been understood as a social obligation—an institution designed mainly for economic security and procreation. Today, marriage is understood mainly as a path toward self-fulfillment."[1]

Paul Amato, another prominent authority on the subject of

marriage, describes the transition from a pre-1960s "institutional marriage" regulated by social norms, public opinion, law and religion to an "individualistic marriage" today. In an institutional marriage, Amato writes that "spouses were expected not only to conform to traditional standards of behavior, but also to sacrifice their personal goals, if necessary, for the sake of the marriage." In contrast, in the modern era, "self-development and personal fulfillment [have replaced] mutual satisfaction and successful team effort as the basis of marriage."[2]

According to Amato, one of the advantages of the institutional marriage is that "men and women participated in an institution that was larger and more significant than themselves," whereas our current focus on personal happiness makes it more likely that marriages will fail because of "the inevitable disappointment that occurs when people's expectations meet reality." Amato suggests that marital happiness should not be part of the definition of marital success or quality. In his view, a successful, high-quality marriage is one that lasts until one of the spouses dies, whether the spouses were madly in love with one another or praying for one another's demise.

In this paradigm, if Barbara and William have an "individualistic marriage" and spend fifteen happy years together followed by two unhappy years and then divorce, their marriage is a failure. On the other hand, if they have an "institutional marriage" and spend fifteen happy years together followed by another twenty years of misery before William dies of leukemia, their marriage is a success. (Interestingly, the "individualistic marriage" could also have been counted as a success if William had died of leukemia the week before their divorce was finalized.)

The beauty of the institutional marriage from the Defective Cow's perspective is that participants don't expect to be happy. In fact, people who seek personal fulfillment in an institutional marriage are considered foolish and small-minded. This means that the Defective Cow can start by telling Barbara that there's something wrong with her because she doesn't want to have sex with William, and if that doesn't work, she can tell Barbara that she needs to focus on something bigger and more important than her own happiness. She can tell Barbara that marriage is an economic and child-rearing institution, and only petty, misguided people believe that marriage should generate happiness.

> Though marriage experts claim that humans were until recently quite rational about marriage, our investigations have uncovered historical voices suggesting an occult aspiration for preeminence of love in marriage. Sources include William Shakespeare, Jane Austen, John Donne, Elizabeth Barrett Browning and others. Browning wrote:
>
> > "I love thee to the depth and breadth and height
> > My soul can reach, when feeling out of sight
> > For the ends of Being and ideal Grace."[3]
>
> Possibly she felt differently after she married Robert Browning, but this doesn't sound like the longing for an "institutional marriage" to us!

The problem with the Defective Cow's argument is that the old-fashioned expectations of an institutional marriage don't fit well in modern Western culture. Marriage has become a choice, because the alternatives to marriage are not as bleak as they once were. Women don't have to be married in order to prosper economically, be sexually active, or even have children.

To look at the business-partner marriage model in the twenty-first century, we have designed a thought experiment about a woman named Jill. Jill is a single mother (by choice) with an infant and a toddler. Jill would like to stay home and look after her children, but she needs to work to support them. Jill decides to open a small daycare, thus earning money while still spending time with her children. Her business grows, and she decides to hire additional help. She brings in her friend Fred, who recently lost his job. Fred is a solid business partner; he is responsible, hardworking and polite.

One morning, Jill is bursting with happy news to share with Fred.

"Fred!" she says. "I have met the love of my life!"

"Sorry," says Fred, "you have to tell him goodbye."

"What??" replies Jill. "What could you possibly mean?"

"Well, we are in business together, and you can't be with another man."

Jill checks with her lawyer, her priest and her mother, and they all agree with Fred.

The next day after work, Fred puts his hand under Jill's skirt.

"What are you doing?" Jill asks angrily.

"We are in an institutional relationship," says Fred, "and so it's your job to take care of my needs."

When Jill complains about this incident to her friend Cindy, Cindy buys her a book called *How to Have Smoking Hot Sex in Your Institutional Relationship*, and suggests that Jill adjust her attitude to be more realistic.

This is a ridiculous example, but the problem is not the example—the problem is that we are living in a confused society. We tell unhappy married couples that their expectations are too high, and that they shouldn't expect passion or great love from marriage. At the same time, we tell them that they can't go *looking* for passion or great love elsewhere. Then, realizing that we have put them in a bind by telling them that they must live passionless lives, we completely negate our first point by reassuring them that with the right therapist or book or attitude, Jill can have a wonderfully passionate sex life with Fred just by working at it (and if she fails, she is defective).

The implication is that people are not being realistic or reasonable if they expect more from marriage than a spouse who can help to pay the mortgage and raise the children without complaining. And yet our society also makes it clear that spouses should *want* to have sex, at least semi-regularly. In fact, our society believes that spouses should care so deeply for one another that they never, ever want to have sex with anyone else.

Our culture has created two views of marriage: 1. Marriage is a business partnership, and passion shouldn't be expected; 2. Marriage is the ultimate expression of deep love and passion. A case can be made for either view of marriage, but the two views are essentially incompatible. If marriage is a business, we shouldn't treat people like they are defective if they don't desire their spouses, or if they fall head over heels for someone else. If marriage is about deeply loving and desiring one another, then we shouldn't tell people that they are whiners when they complain that these things are missing from their marriages. Our collective lack of clarity about these two incompatible views of marriage leads to seriously confused advice for people considering divorce (and marriage, for that matter). This blatantly irrational Sacred Cow should be trivial to tip, and yet it leaves many people Cowed by feelings of guilt and inadequacy. Let's help them out by giving the Defective Cow a little shove.

Udderly Personal

I met my husband when I was sixteen, and he was the only man I had ever been with. We both thought that something was wrong with me, because I was not interested in sex. My husband insisted that we go to the gynecologist, who said that nothing physical was wrong with me, but maybe I had suffered some sort of abuse as a child. I insisted that I had never been abused, but my husband wanted me to see a psychologist. The whole time, I really thought that I was abnormal. Now that we are divorced and I have a new man in my life, I know that there was never anything wrong with me at all. It wasn't sex that didn't interest me; it was my husband who didn't interest me.

—Perfectly Normal in New England

Mad (Cow) Libs

The Defective Cow doesn't just want people to feel defective for being unhappily married; she wants to make sure that we all know that divorced people are defective. The influence of the Defective Cow can be seen when society judges people and situations involving divorce more harshly than analogous situations in which marriage is not an issue. To illustrate such double standards, we have devised a game of "mad cow libs.". In each of the following paragraphs, we will substitute the words in italics, and you can see how you react differently in each case:

> Your younger brother surprises you when he calls you to tell you that he is planning to _marry_ Anita! You have always had some serious reservations about Anita, although you can see that she has some good qualities too. Your brother tells you that he is very _happy_.

Would you tell your brother to wait and give it more thought, and do you share your reservations about Anita with him? Or do you decide that only he knows what makes him happy, and it's not your place to meddle in matters of the heart? Now try this:

> Your younger brother surprises you when he calls you to tell you that he is planning to _divorce_ Anita! You have always had some serious reservations about Anita, although you can see that she has some good qualities too. Your brother tells you that he is very _unhappy_.

Okay, now do you tell your brother to slow down, think it over, and give it more time? Or do you assume that only he knows what will make him happy and applaud him for making a hard decision? Be honest. We are betting that you would do the first, because that's what most of us would probably do. It's not particularly rational, however, to treat these two situations so differently. Marriage and divorce are both enormous decisions, and so you should probably try to advise your brother in both cases or trust him to make the right decision in both cases. He is not logically more likely to make a mistake about divorce than he is to make a mistake about marriage. In fact, he probably knows a lot more about the Anita he is divorcing than the Anita he married, so one could argue that he is better equipped to decide about divorce than about marriage.

Here is another example:

> Your friend Julie has been _living with_ Brian for the past four years. While they have a comfortable relationship, she doesn't think that he is the right partner for her. Lately, she feels that she is just going through the motions, and that their relationship is dead.

Do you encourage Julie to stick it out with Brian for the rest of her life? To have children with him? Do you feel that she would be a quitter if she left Brian?

Now substitute the words "living with" for "married." Does that change how you talk to Julie? You are probably more likely to tell her to persevere and to reassure her that although everyone has ups and downs, things always get better. Rationally you know that Julie is no more likely to be happy with Brian whether they are married or not. If you push her to stay with Brian in the case where they are married but not in the case where they are unmarried, then you are presumably valuing the commitment more highly than her happiness. This is not hypocritical as long as you are honest with Julie about your motives. However, if you say, "Things will get better," in one case and not the other, then you are channeling the Defective Cow and her double standards.

Try this one:

> Paula is on a first date with Vikram after they met on an Internet dating site. Paula mentions her recent trip to Venice, and Vikram says, "My _ex-girlfriend_ was Italian, so I have spent quite a lot of time in Italy. Venice is one of my favorite cities."

What does Paula think? Perhaps she wonders whether Vikram's ex-girlfriend is beautiful or whether Vikram speaks Italian. Perhaps she is happy that they have this in common, and she fantasizes that one day they might travel to Venice together. Now substitute the word "ex-girlfriend" with "ex-wife." Does Paula now see him differently? Does she wonder what is wrong with Vikram that his wife didn't want him or that he can't sustain a committed relationship? Does she consider him damaged goods?

These two situations are not perfectly equivalent, because Vikram's level of commitment to a wife would have been different from his level of commitment to a girlfriend. Keeping promises is something that is valued by our society. However, knowing nothing about the reasons for the breakup in either case, it is unfair to Vikram to treat him as defective only because he is divorced.

Okay, here is the last one:

> Your friend Antonio got _a tattoo of a skull and the word "death" on his neck_ when he was twenty. Now he is forty, and he deeply regrets having made what he now considers to be a rash decision at an age when he couldn't possibly know what sort of a person he would be at age forty. He tells you that he is considering _having the tattoo removed_.

We won't insult your intelligence by pretending that marriage is in the same category as a tattoo. It's interesting, though, that we agree with Antonio that the "death" tattoo is more prophetic than fashionable at his age, but we would probably take a different attitude if it were his marriage that he considered to be a mistake. If we're willing to cut him slack on his tattoo removal, we should be even more understanding about divorce—his wife might have changed in unexpected ways over twenty years, unlike his tattoo.

> I've been married three times—and each time I married the right person.
>
> —Margaret Mead

"But you seem so happy!"

"You two seem so happy. Why would you throw that away?" This is a refrain heard by many couples considering divorce. Their families and friends are genuinely shocked that things could be so bad in the marriage that a solution as radical as divorce would be required. What this statement shows is the large gulf that often exists between how marriages look from the outside and how they feel to the participants. It also suits the Defective Cow's agenda that people generally perceive married people to be happy and divorced people to be deserving of pity. It's easier for her to convince you that divorced people are defective if you are already feeling sorry for them.

Imagine that you have a friend, Susie, who is unhappy in her marriage and considering a divorce. Susie comes to you in tears, looking to you for support and guidance. Susie tells you that she is increasingly miserable in her marriage, and that nothing she tries makes things any better. She cannot imagine staying with her husband, Larry, but she cannot imagine being divorced, either. You run through both scenarios in your mind and try to imagine two different future Susies. Married Susie looks a lot like the Susie you have known for the past ten years; she is not very happy, but she will continue to enjoy Larry's fabulous Thanksgiving turkey with cranberry relish every year and tend the difficult flower beds in her shady yard. Divorced Susie lives alone in a one-bedroom apartment with her cat and a subscription to Netflix. It's always raining outside. Divorced Susie seems so sad.

Is it possible, as we hover peering through the window of Divorced Susie's apartment, that she is actually happy? Divorced Susie may finally be able to watch *Sleepless in Seattle* without having to trade barbed remarks with Larry. She may be completely relaxed, free of the cold hostility that pervaded her old house. She may be enjoying her steaming cup of tea and her cat curled in her lap. Maybe her adoring new chef boyfriend is on his way home from work with leftover pork medallions in mustard sauce that he will tenderly feed to her while sharing the stories of his last shift. Maybe Susie is thinking, "If I were back in that wretched mausoleum with Larry, I would be on my way to bed now to avoid having to spend another minute with him and that damned Rottweiler."

We have a strong bias towards believing that people are less happy after divorce that is based much more in our collective failure of imagination than in reality. One reason is that we assume single people are less happy than those in relationships. The evidence for this is weak, but let's say for argument's sake that it is true. It is still a poor argument with respect to divorce, since few divorcé(e)s remain single for the rest of their lives.

You would only apply this argument to Susie if you believed that no man other than Larry would want to be with her. It is also a poor argument because you already know that Susie is unhappy. If she is on the unhappy end of the spectrum for married people, isn't it possible that she would be better off as an average happy single person?

Another reason why we might want to steer Susie towards staying in her marriage is that the process of divorcing is almost universally painful. There is no doubt that if you compared the average happiness of people in the middle of a divorce to their happiness three years prior, you would conclude that marriage makes people happier than divorce. This is also a specious argument, similar to telling someone with gangrene that they shouldn't have an amputation because they will feel pain after surgery. Life changes are difficult, but not making changes can sometimes be even more catastrophic.

The scientific evidence that divorce makes people unhappy

The point of Susie's story is that many of us unknowingly have the prejudiced view that divorce makes people less happy than marriage, and that prejudiced belief represents a Sacred Cow. Some of you may now be thinking, "But it is not just a prejudiced belief, because I have heard about studies showing that people are less happy after divorce!" True, many self-help books and resources aimed at preventing divorce will quote studies that supposedly prove that divorce makes people miserable. This is a murky area of quasi-scientific research, and the results of studies tend to reinforce each investigator's preconceived ideas. Thus, those who believe that divorce is a destabilizing life change with no clear-cut long-term effects tend to discover that divorce does not impact happiness, while those who believe that life is a long downhill slide after divorce find the opposite.

For those who wish to demonstrate that divorce is bad, one of the go-to references is a review article published by Paul

Amato in 2000. Here is what Amato had to say on the subject: "A large number of studies published during the 1990s found that divorced individuals, compared with married individuals, experience lower levels of psychological well-being, including lower happiness, more symptoms of psychological distress, and poorer self-concepts (Aseltine & Kessler, 1993; Davies et al., 1997; Demo & Acock, 1996b; Kitson, 1992; Lorenz et al., 1997; Marks, 1996; Mastekaasa, 1994a, 1994b, 1995; Robins & Regier, 1991; Ross, 1995; Shapiro, 1996; Simon, 1998; Simon & Marcussen, 1999; Simons & Associates, 1996; Umberson & Williams, 1993; White, 1992)."[4]

That is an impressive number of citations, and the statement about divorced individuals being less happy sounds awfully definitive. Did all of these studies really show that divorce causes people to have sad lives? Well, not exactly. Actually, not even close. Let's discuss the first reference (Aseltine & Kessler, 1993)[5] so that you can see what the researchers actually did. For analyses of the remaining references, please visit our website **SacredCowsTheBook.com.**

Aseltine and Kessler surveyed couples in Detroit in 1985, asking each individual to rate his or her happiness over the last 30 days on a 4-point scale. Three years later, the same individuals were re-surveyed. During that period, 4% of the people had separated or divorced (61 people in total), and 0.04% of people had remarried (6 people in total). It turned out that some in the separated/divorced group were happier and some were sadder, but on average, they reported a greater decrease in their happiness than did the married people.

Let's think about this for a moment. The couples picked for this study were not chosen because they were on the brink of divorce. Even if some couples were ready to split up the day after the first survey was administered, the absolute longest anybody could have been separated by the time the study ended was three years minus one day. Most of the couples must have separated more recently than that, up to and including the day before the second and final survey. That isn't a lot of time to get over the trauma of splitting up, particularly given how long and drawn-out the process of divorce tends to be. Hurt feelings, anxiety, anger and uncertainty are the norm in the months and sometimes years surrounding divorce; it therefore seems unfair to try to measure the happiness of someone who is freshly separated or divorced and then extrapolate that feeling to the rest of their lives.

Setting aside for the moment the question about whether the researchers were measuring the correct outcome, how much of a difference between the groups did they actually find? Were the divorced people really, really depressed compared to the married people? It turns out that their reported happiness decreased one quarter of one standard deviation more than the married group. To put this in perspective, imagine that you were studying obesity in American men, and you had a "fat" cohort that was one quarter of one standard deviation heavier than the "skinny" cohort. The difference between the groups would be about 7.5 lbs. This finding might be statistically significant, but you would have a hard time arguing that it was a life-altering difference in weight.

What did the six people who got remarried have to say about their happiness? They were happy. In fact, the increase in their happiness was far greater in magnitude than the decrease in happiness for the rest of the divorced group. (This is an important observation, because many studies do not include remarried people in the "divorced" group.) It's impossible to conclude anything at all with such a small group of remarried people, but it is clear that remarriage rates need to be taken into account when analyzing outcomes for divorce.

This is only the first example of the studies cited in this reference, but we think that you will agree that it in no way demonstrates "that divorced individuals, compared with married individuals, experience lower levels of psychological well-being, including lower happiness, more symptoms of psychological distress, and poorer self-concepts." If you visit our website, you will see that the remaining studies do no better.

Good studies about divorce are lacking, but researchers who study divorce should not be accused of lack of effort. It may be impossible to design a study to determine whether any given person would be meaningfully happier if he or she stayed married or got divorced. One of the reasons for this is that it doesn't do any good to compare contented married couples with divorcing couples. People who are happily married are not saying to themselves, "Hmm, maybe I will get divorced this year." Likewise, people who are seriously contemplating divorce are not choosing between two fabulous options. A comparison between the happiness of contented spouses and spouses going through a divorce is entirely uninformative.

To be informative, a study would have to compare people who are equally unhappy in their marriages but make different decisions about sticking it out or leaving. Nobody has yet figured out how to do that. Furthermore, it would be nearly impossible to advise an individual based on the results of even the best-performed study. If you live in Oregon, and we told you that people in Oregon are 10% more likely to suffer from depression than people in Massachusetts, would you pick up your life and move to Massachusetts based on that information? Of course not. Similarly, even if someone convinced you divorced people are on average 10% less happy than married people, that wouldn't help you to decide what to do in your specific circumstances.

This is not to say that divorce is easy, or that divorced people have been scientifically proven to be just as happy as or happier than married people. All we are saying is that nobody has convincingly demonstrated that choosing to stay married rather than choosing to divorce results in a happier life. Furthermore, even if divorced people are less happy on average than married people, you need to make decisions about your life based on your individual circumstances, not based on averages. So the next time someone tells you that choosing divorce has been scientifically proven to destroy happiness, you can give that Sacred Cow a shove and watch it topple right over.

Conclusion

You have now learned to recognize the Defective Cow in all of her many guises. As you can see, she is a wily creature. The Defective Cow tries to make people feel defective for being unhappy about their marriages, and she also tries to convince them that getting divorced would only prove that they are even more defective than she originally thought. Nobody should be Cowed by this judgmental bovine. There are many good reasons to get married and to stay married, but shame, embarrassment and self-reproach are not among them.

References
1. Popenoe, D. (1996). *Life without Father*. New York, NY: Simon and Schuster.
2. Amato, P. R. (2007). *Alone Together: How Marriage in America is Changing*. Cambrigde, MA: Harvard University Press.
3. Browning, E.B. (1850). *Sonnets from the Portuguese*. New York, NY: St Martin's Press.
4. Amato, P. R. (2000). The consequences of divorce for adults and children. *Journal of Marriage and the Family*, 62, 1269-1287.
5. Aseltine R.H., Kessler R.C. (1993). Marital disruption and depression in a community sample. *Journal of Health and Social Behavior*, 34(3), 237-251.

CHAPTER FIVE
The Innocent
Victim Cow

I was the type of kid who would say, "Hey, look at the bright side! We'll have two Christmases."
—*Will Ferrell*

Meet the Cow

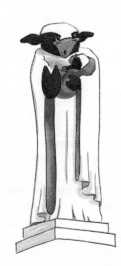

The Innocent Victim Cow is a master manipulator. She pulls on heartstrings and exploits protective parental instincts to get people to do what she wants, which, like all the Cows, is for everyone to stay married. This Cow's Achilles' heel is her impressive teetering pile of fake data that leaves her vulnerable to being pushed over with a light intellectual tap.

Caveat: The Cow in this chapter is not that children will find the process of divorce difficult and sad. Children do suffer when their parents divorce. The Innocent Victim Cow represents the idea that children whose parents stay in a bad marriage have measurably happier, more productive and more fulfilled lives than they would have had if their parents had chosen to divorce.

It's the kids who suffer

Jason was an ambitious and talented young man who seemed destined for success. Medea fell in love with him while he was still struggling to obtain the Golden Fleece. She promised to help him if he would marry her, and Jason could see how much of an asset Medea could be with her talents and connections. Plus, she was hot. Medea came through on her promise to propel Jason to greatness, although sadly at the expense of her own father and brother. Jason and Medea had two children together, and both doted on them. While their children were still young, however, Jason left Medea for another woman. Medea was so beside herself with pain and rage that she murdered both of her own children to punish Jason for his betrayal.

The ancient Greek poet Euripides certainly earned his label "great tragedian" with this story about Medea. Murdering children is pretty extreme, but Euripides may have been making the point that it is the innocent victims who suffer when marriages crumble. This is, in fact, the strongest argument our society advances for why people should stay married: "Divorce will hurt the innocent children, and you certainly love your children. Are you such a monster that you are willing to sacrifice

Udderly Personal

Before I got divorced, I felt a bit like a ghost at home. My wife was so much in charge of everything related to the kids, and she was so activity oriented with them that I didn't feel like I had a real role. After our marriage soured, things got even worse because I didn't enjoy being home at all. Now that I share custody with my ex-wife, I have become much closer to my daughters. We have more downtime together that we all enjoy, and we share an intimacy that I treasure so much more than the time that I have lost with them due to shared custody. I may only see them half the time, but it is precious time that I look forward to and savor, and I know that my children do too.

—Born-Again Dad in Denver

their well-being for your own freedom?"

Obviously, this is a highly emotional argument designed to elicit guilt. Parents care deeply about the welfare of their children, and there is nothing like a big dollop of parental guilt to convince them to sacrifice their own self-interests for the interests of their children. This is why "staying married for the children" is so common that it has become a cliché in our society.

Since cultural assumptions and Sacred Cows go hoof in hand, it seems probable that there is a Sacred Cow sneakily grazing in the midst of all of that parental emotion. It is time to ask ourselves the following questions: What it is that we assume will happen to children in the event of their parents' divorcing, and what is the basis for believing these things?

The happiness question

Before we move on to the question about children's lives being ruined by divorce, let's first address the issue of happiness. Are children made unhappy by their parents' divorcing? We don't think that any of us need scientific studies to answer that question. The answer is yes, usually, at least for the short term. Most children are made unhappy to some degree and for some length of time when their parents divorce. Divorce is a difficult life change. If two people are unhappily married but want to prevent their children from feeling at least temporarily sad about the breakup of their marriage, they shouldn't get divorced. Of course they may be bringing other future unhappiness to their children by remaining married, and they may also be depriving their children of opportunities that could have come to them through a different family structure. Life is full of joys and sadness, and each couple has to decide for themselves whether staying married would on balance bring their children the most long-term happiness. Short-term happiness can be easily predicted (If I kick you hard in the shins, you will be unhappy), but long-term happiness is sufficiently difficult to measure and predict that even the boldest social scientists rarely offer formulae for ensuring lifelong happiness for children. We would venture that nobody knows with certainty whether their children's long-term happiness will be greater if their parents stay married or divorce.

> # WARNING!
> ## Statistics ahead. Proceed with caution.

Lies, damn lies and statistics

Since happiness is so difficult to measure, and since nobody has really addressed the issue of long-term happiness of children after divorce, what are examples of statistics reported in this situation? One frequently cited statistic is that children of divorced parents are more likely to get divorced themselves when they grow up. When put that way, that does sound rather sad. You might think, "If I set a bad example by getting divorced, then my child will not have a model of a committed relationship to follow, and that will cause him to be incapable of staying in a marriage himself." Or maybe you will think, "If my child doesn't have the experience of a nuclear family, then she is going to choose a spouse for all the wrong reasons, and her marriage won't last." There are many interpretations or assumptions that you could make given that one statistic. But what if we reported the exact same fact with a different spin: "If you don't have the courage to leave an unhappy marriage, your child is statistically more likely to get stuck in a similar situation when he becomes an adult." Obviously, how arguments are framed matters just as much as the statistics themselves.

Correlation is not causation

One of the reasons why statistics can cause us to arrive at the wrong conclusions is that statistics generally tell us nothing about cause and effect. Correlation does not equal causation, and further, causation is not as interesting as root causation. For example, suppose a study has shown that wealth and horse ownership are highly correlated. If you didn't know that correlation does not equal causation, you might buy a horse so that you could get richer. Let's say that the study also showed that the most common characteristic that wealthy people share is that they're paid well. That may be true; it may even be true that being paid well causes wealth, but that statistic isn't very helpful to you if you want to get rich. It doesn't tell you anything about root causation, or "*why* are they paid well?" Using that same logic, if we share with you the statistic that children of divorced parents are more likely to get divorced themselves, this might well tell you absolutely nothing. How? Let's break that down and see how that might work.

Let's say, for argument's sake, that people with poor impulse control are more likely to get divorced than people with strong impulse control. And let's say that impulse control passes from parents to children both genetically and via children's patterning of parents' behavior. If Mom and Dad with poor impulse control get divorced, and their child Olivia (who also has poor impulse control) gets divorced when she grows up, can we conclude that Olivia's parents' divorce caused her divorce? No, we can't. In this thought experiment, the real problem is poor impulse control, and Olivia would have had a high likelihood of divorcing whether her parents had stayed together or not. To blame Olivia's divorce on her parents' divorce is like saying that my getting sunburned caused you to become sunburned also, when the actual cause is beaming down on us both from the sky.

Let's look at another example. One of the best-recognized and most easily measured factors known to be associated with divorce is low family income. Children of poor families also (on average) do worse in school than children of wealthy families. Poor children tend to grow up to be poor adults, and they are therefore more likely to suffer from negative effects of poverty throughout their lives. Since poor parents are also (on average) more likely to divorce than wealthy parents, a researcher could conclude that children whose parents divorce do worse in school than children whose parents do not divorce, and be perfectly correct. This is no more meaningful, however, than if the researcher had said, "Children who never vacation in France are more likely to drop out of school than children who have visited at least one French art museum." If our society is being fair and unbiased, we should admit that implying causation in both of these statements is reasonable or that it is nonsense in both cases. Yet we have politicians advocating spending tax dollars to promote marriage but not to send children to Paris. Why not?

Experimenter's bias

The reason why politicians advocate for marriage but not for Paris is because they get paid to listen to their constituents; they don't get paid to be scientific. What about researchers though? Surely they are motivated to be unbiased. Well, yes and no. Most researchers care about the truth, but they also have innate biases and external pressures. They may receive funding from organizations motivated to find harmful effects associated with divorce or positive effects associated with marriage. They are also a lot more likely to get their work published and talked about on TV if they come up with conclusions like "Divorce causes children to become drug mules!" than conclusions like "Well, it's very complicated, and we really can't say for certain whether or how divorce affects children's success in life." Professors who don't publish papers soon become ex-professors, and so there is great incentive to find and report the kinds of outcomes that the government, the journals, the press and the funders want to hear.

> **Helpful tip:** If your eyes have glazed over and the word "statistics" is making you queasy, you can skip to the next chapter, which is entirely mathematics-free. If you are enjoying the geek-fest, we have more examples of scientific stumbling blocks below.

Selection bias

One of the biggest problems with studying the effects of divorce on children is that the people who choose to get divorced are not (on average) the same kinds of people as those who choose to stay married. We have already hinted at this issue in the discussion about causation above. We know, for instance, that people who get married at a younger age have a higher likelihood of divorce than those who marry later. People who have mood disorders, substance abuse problems or personality disorders are more likely to divorce. Wealthy or highly religious individuals are less likely to divorce. People who live in Alabama are more likely to divorce than people who live in Massachusetts. We could go on, but you get the idea.

The upshot of these groups of people being different from one another (on average) is that researchers end up trying to compare apples with oranges when they study children of divorced versus intact families. When researchers make this kind of mistake, it is called "selection bias," and it can cause investigators to arrive at erroneous conclusions. For instance, let's say that you wanted to study the factors that enable a successful career in professional hockey in order to write an advice book for aspiring hockey players. You could choose to compare the population of Canada, which has a high percentage of successful players, with the population of Mexico, which has a lower percentage of professional hockey players. You might then conclude that consumption of tasty food is inversely correlated with the likelihood of playing professional hockey and recommend to hockey hopefuls that they immediately adopt a diet of bland food covered in maple syrup. This unfortunate conclusion would have arisen from the fact that you chose to compare two populations of people who are very different from one another in more ways than the food they eat. (For instance, Mexicans are a lot more excited about fútbol than they are about hockey!)

Controlling for selection bias

Since selection bias is an enormous problem for all divorce research, investigators try to come up with ways to control for this. One option is to use standard regression models. This means that after you come up with the result of your study (for example, children with divorced parents fare 20% more poorly in school than their peers from intact families), you then go back and try to factor in all of the things you think might bias your sample. This makes your sample smaller and your conclusion weaker and weaker until sometimes it disappears altogether, particularly if you studied a relatively small group of people. Once you "adjust" for the fact that divorced parents have less schooling themselves, you may decide that the children in your study actually fared only 10% worse. Then if you factor in the differences in income between the two groups, your difference may dwindle to 5%. And so on.

Now we will venture further out into the confusing land of basic statistics where even some tenured professors fear to go. Here is the reality. If you want to see whether divorce and poor school performance are correlated, you can normalize the problem with respect to family income and parental education. If you cared to do it properly, you would need to know the correlation between income and education level also so as not to over- or underadjust (if those two factors were positively or negatively correlated, respectively). This is a little confusing, perhaps, but not mind-bending. Here's the hard part. What if the factors to adjust for are not clear-cut and well-understood things like income and education but rather things that are difficult to quantify, like job stress and empathy? Do you know how correlated those two things are? We don't, and we're pretty sure anyone who says they know is making it up. Moreover, while it's easy to measure income and education, nobody has a job stress meter or an empathy meter. So when divorce is related not to two factors like income and education, but to literally hundreds of factors including mental illness, job stress, religious beliefs, health, impulse control and so forth, we give you permission to be a little skeptical about whether the researchers have controlled for all of these.

We spoke with an expert in the field of family research about study design, and he agreed that selection bias may be the greatest obstacle that social science research has to contend with. Professor of Sociology Philip Cohen told us, "Anyone who tells you that they are controlling for selection is not, really. They can't. We don't measure the things that cause both divorce and problems for children. If you have a difficult personality and don't get along well with other people, you are more likely to get divorced, and your children are more likely to grow up miserable. We don't have a way of capturing that. That's just one easy example of something we don't even try to measure when we study these things. There are lots of things like that."

The ways in which people choose to try to control for selection bias may ironically be driven, at least in part, by their own preconceived notions about what the study should show. Researchers who want to show the largest possible difference in outcomes between children of divorced families and intact families generally make no attempt to control for selection bias. Researchers who want to be a little bit more scientific about it, but are still hoping for an interesting study result, will control for only some of the factors known to be associated with divorce. This is true of the largest study we could find that looks at children's educational outcomes following family disruption.[1] The authors made a big deal of controlling for several demographic factors such as parental education, but they left income out of their analysis. At the end of their long academic paper, the authors parenthetically state that if you included parental earnings in the analysis, then the effects of divorce on children's educational attainment "fall, as might be expected." Yet for some reason, they did not provide readers with the analysis that included income. Presumably the paper would have been hard to publish if the results showed no effect of divorce on children's school performance, which is why they chose to sweep this issue under the rug.

> ## Udderly Personal
>
> *I don't mind that my parents are divorced. What really bugs me is when a friend asks, "Where are you and your parents going for vacation?" and when I say, "My parents are divorced but I'm going skiing with my dad," my friend gets all embarrassed and sorry for asking the question. I have to explain that it's fine that my parents are divorced, and I love going on vacations with both my parents ... Plus I get twice as many vacations as any other kid I know! It's so weird that other people feel embarrassed or sorry for me that my parents are divorced. What's up with that?*
>
> —Puzzled Pre-Teen in Punxsutawney

The cure for selection bias

If it is beginning to sound like you can't trust the results of any study confounded by selection bias, well, that's probably right. The Federal Drug Administration would never approve a drug that was studied in the same way that divorce is studied. That is because the FDA knows that the results of such investigations can never be considered definitive. So what is the cure for selection bias? The best solution is a randomized study. These are the sorts of trials that drug companies need to conduct if they hope to be able to sell drugs to consumers. Why don't these kinds of studies exist in divorce research?

To conduct such a study, researchers would need to randomly assign a large number of married parents to two groups: one where everyone gets divorced and one where everyone stays married. Imagine participating in a trial where you were told, "You will get an envelope in the mail, selected at random, that will tell you whether you need to get divorced next week or whether you must stay married for at least the next five years. Then we will test your kids every year to see how they are faring." Maybe you would agree to such a study if you were paid *really* well, but who is going to fork over millions (possibly billions) of dollars to conduct such research?

Why you shouldn't listen to a social scientist about whether to get a divorce

Social scientist Philip Cohen says that you should not pay attention to people like him when you are trying to make a decision about your family life. Here is what Cohen had to say:

"People want to see research that proves that what they are doing is okay, or what other people are doing is not okay. There are real problems with applying research findings to an individual life; it's a disastrous, calamitous problem in our society that social science gets written up with headlines in the second person, like 'Why Your Boss Is Making You a Republican.' My boss is *not* making me a Republican. I am never going to be a Republican. But some study may find a correlation between Republican bosses and Republican employees, and then it gets written up as a misleading headline.

"The best research on divorce and child outcomes does not explain much of the variance in child outcomes. This is because the people doing the research don't know that much about the people they are studying. They might know some good, important variables like age, sex, race, income, or education. However, if you actually know the people involved, the specifics of the case are going to be more important than everything else. If a really good study on child well-being explained 20% or 30 of the variance, that would be phenomenal. But if you know the people involved, you might know exactly what is going to happen, with virtually 100% certainty. No study should be the basis for overruling what you know about yourself or your loved ones."

What do the studies supposedly show?

Having established that there are no truly rigorous studies of children and divorce, what do published studies purportedly demonstrate? We have already mentioned the sociologist Paul Amato and his summaries of divorce studies that are so highly cited. In a meta-analysis of 67 studies from the 1990s,[2] Amato reported that more than half of published comparisons showed no statistical differences between children of divorced and married parents. To be fair, that doesn't necessarily mean that differences weren't present; it simply means that they weren't detected. Amato noted that the best studies were the least likely to show significant differences, however, suggesting that design flaws prejudiced the numbers in favor of finding differences, not in favor of finding no differences. Of the studies that did find statistical differences in outcomes for children such as academic achievement and conduct, the average size of the difference was about one quarter of one standard deviation.

Interestingly, this is the same magnitude of difference that one of the previously discussed studies of happiness demonstrated. To put this in perspective, think about it this way: You are told that a study shows that men who live in Boston are tall, and men who live in New York City are of average height. The difference between the two groups of men is one quarter of one standard deviation. That means that on average, men in New York are 5 feet 10 inches tall, whereas men in Boston are on average 5 feet 10 and three quarters inches tall. When you meet a man who is 6 feet tall, can you predict with any reasonable certainty whether he is from Boston or New York? Of course not. Similarly, when a child is failing academically or having difficulties socially, you could not with any reliability guess whether his parents are divorced or not *even if these studies had been properly designed.*

So, when people tell you that "studies show" that kids do worse when their parents divorce, they are failing to recognize that the vast majority of research in this area is contaminated by selection bias and other design flaws. They are also failing to mention that most studies detect no differences between children raised in divorced vs. intact families, and that even when differences are detected, they are miniscule. There are lots of reasons to think hard before deciding to divorce, but guilt about disadvantaging children should not be one of them. When the Innocent Victim Cow claims that divorce is scientifically proven to ruin children's lives, we tell her thanks, but we have already herd enough.

Udderly Personal

I grew up in the perfect family, and my parents had the perfect marriage until last year. Three months after I left home for college, they filed for divorce. I am the youngest of two daughters, and it is obvious that they had been planning to divorce for years, but they waited until we were both out of the house. I know that I should feel grateful, and I guess I do, but that gratitude is completely buried under other feelings. I still feel the sickening disorientation of the day when our parents told us that they were getting a divorce. I am sad that they split up, but I am more horrified when I wonder how much of my life (months, years, or more) were a complete charade being played out by my parents to fool us into believing they were happy. I also feel terribly guilty that my parents stayed married simply because of my sister and me, despite being miserable. My parents thought they were doing the right thing for us by staying married until we were adults … but although I am eternally grateful for the love they have shown us, I don't want the burden of my debt; I did not want them to trade their happiness for what they thought was a happier childhood for me.

—Regretful at Rutgers

Conclusion

While the Innocent Victim Cow deserves to be tipped, the idea that divorce causes pain cannot be entirely disregarded. Divorce is upsetting to children, and some children grow up to feel that they are emotionally crippled because of their parents' divorce. (Of course, some children also grow up to feel that they are emotionally crippled because their parents stayed married too long.) Even children who view the changes resulting from divorce as positive still have to suffer through the upheaval of changing family structure. The effects of divorce on children should be taken seriously, and parents should make every effort to mitigate the pain for their children. That said, parents should not be told that their children's long-term happiness and success will be jeopardized if they divorce. There is no respectable evidence that (all other things being equal) divorce meaningfully impacts the sort of adult a child will become. Moreover, even if good quality studies existed, decisions about divorce need to be made based upon the individual details of each situation, not based on some faulty notion of the law of averages.

References

1. Steele, F., Sigle-Rushton, W., Kravdal, Ø. (2009). Consequences of family disruption on children's educational outcomes in Norway. *Demography*, 46(3), 553-574.
2. Amato, P.R. (2001). Children of Divorce in the 1990s: An update of the Amato and Keith (1991) meta-analysis. *Journal of Family Psychology*, 15, 355-370.

CHAPTER SIX
The One True Cow

One should always be in love. That is the reason
one should never marry.
—*Oscar Wilde*

Meet the Cow

The One True Cow is confused—she is
both a romantic and cynic. She believes
in true love for people who aren't married
and uses it as a pleasant cattle prod to get
everyone to the altar. However, for those
who end up unhappy in their marriages,
she insists that true love is an illusion.

Caveat: This chapter does not prove
whether or not true love exists, nor does
it provide any formula for finding it. We
are only taking this Cow to task for being
two-faced and making people feel unnecessarily bad for desiring
true love after marriage as much as they were encouraged to
desire true love before marriage.

True love is ...

"Feeling that your life has no meaning or purpose
without him."

"Pure happiness."

"An overwhelming feeling of bliss every time you see her face."

"Space and time measured by the heart."

"Never having to say you're sorry."

"A many-splendored thing."

"A candle whose flame can never be extinguished."

"Taking out the garbage without being asked."

These were just a few of the answers that popped up in our Google search page when we asked the question, "What is true love?" If you needed to explain to an alien visiting planet Earth the nature of true love, these answers would only confuse and frustrate the poor intergalactic tourist. It is no wonder that so many of us are also confused about this topic.

Many a marriage has been abandoned for lack of true love, and many an unhappy spouse has been chastised for daring to dream of true love. As in religion, there are believers and nonbelievers, and in the interest of full disclosure, we will tell you that we belong to the first group. Our goal is not to proselytize about true love, however, but only to examine cultural attitudes and beliefs that surround true love, and to try to identify any Sacred Cows that may be loitering nearby.

Platonic love

Many among us don't buy into the concept of true love, and for good reason. Nobody can agree about what it looks like, we cannot define it or verify its authenticity, and most of us have serious doubt that "bliss" is what most long-married people experience while watching their spouse take the garbage to the curb. Despite our collective cynicism, however, there is a strong cultural desire for true love that shows clearly in the stories we tell in novels, movies and fairy tales. We still talk today about finding our "other half," but many of us do not realize that this concept originated with Plato. He told the story about how Zeus punished the first humans by cutting each person in half (apparently Zeus didn't mess around when it came to discipline). Each human then longed constantly for his/her other half and sought to be rejoined. Plato tells us that when a person meets the half that is his very own, "something wonderful happens: the two are struck from their senses by love, by a sense of belonging to one another, and by desire, and they don't want to be separated from one another, not even for a moment."

He goes on to say, "These are the people who finish out their lives together and still cannot say what it is they want from one another. No one would think it is the intimacy of sex—that mere sex is the reason each lover takes so great and deep a joy in being with the other. It's obvious that the soul of every lover longs for something else." This, perhaps, is as close a description of true love as we are ever going to get, but it seems worrisomely random, this idea of wandering about until you happen upon your other half. Not to mention the disturbing Zeus-cutting-in-half part.

True love is not a feeling, it's a behavior

Plato described a feeling that many of us have experienced in the head-over-heels adrenaline rush and obsession of new love. The trouble is that we frequently decide weeks or months or years later that we were complete fools to be crazy about *that* particular person, and so it could not have been true love. We tell ourselves and others that what we mistook for true love was mere infatuation, and we hope that next time we can detect the difference.

If we can't trust our feelings on this matter, then perhaps true love has more to do with behaviors. Perhaps true love is some combination of loyalty, self-sacrifice, patience and acts of caring. That seems a bit more solid, something that you can bank on in a long-term relationship. These are important elements of a successful marriage. But if this is true love, what distinguishes it from the love that you feel for your parent or sibling or friend? Is true love just like any other kind of love but with the additional desire for smooching? That degrades the idea of true love, because we want to believe that we have only one true love, or at least that our true love is special and unusual. If true love encompasses everyone we ever cared about and wanted to smooch, then it doesn't seem so special anymore.

Does true love even exist?

Unfortunately, since there's little agreement about the definition of true love, there is no hope for consensus about the existence of true love. Nobody can prove that true love doesn't exist any more than they can prove that leprechauns don't exist. On the

Udderly Personal

I think the idea of "true love" in the traditional sense is outdated, as is the idea that we have only one "soul mate." And, one can learn to un-love someone. The divorce process helps with that. When my ex told me that he wanted out of the marriage—one doesn't really "ask" for a divorce—it came as a complete shock to me. The divorce process lasted for five years, went through two arbitrations, a trial, an appeal, and finally back to the original judge.

In the fifth year, I said "uncle." During those years, I learned to see my ex in ways that I had never before seen him. The nastiness, selfishness and name-calling all helped me to learn not to love him, or to put it in a place so small, dark and deep inside me so as not to be called love at all.

Was he my "true love"? I truly loved him.

At first, I thought I would never love again. Moving on was forced on me, and I did. It opened me up for the next soul mate who would come into my life, someone I truly love. If I should ever move on from this relationship, I know that there are other souls who will come into my life who I will also love truly. The universe is too vast for us to believe that there is only one person for one person for our entire lives.

—Peaceful in Pennsylvania

other hand, while anyone can prove the existence of leprechauns merely by producing one of the cheerful little fellows, it doesn't do much good to say, "I've experienced true love; therefore, I know that it exists!" Self-report does not amount to solid evidence. We are therefore left to conclude that true love may or may not exist, and the One True Cow wants to keep it this way. As you will see in this chapter, the fact that we can neither define true love nor decide whether it is life's highest aspiration or greatest folly results in confusion that the One True Cow can use to her full advantage.

> Love: An obsessive delusion that is cured by marriage
> —Phil Spector

True love is the most important thing ... until it isn't

Perhaps the most confusing message about true love that we receive in our culture is that finding true love should be our highest priority and greatest goal ... until we get married. After we get married, we need to forget all the stuff we were just told about prioritizing true love above all else. Beginning on the wedding day, we need to stop believing that true love exists at all unless we're attaching that feeling to our current spouse.

To illustrate this, think about the standard plot of romantic comedies, where the heroine begins in a relatively unsatisfying relationship (or at the end of a string of unsatisfying relationships) before she falls in love with the handsome male lead. Stumbling blocks are thrown in their path, but the two persevere and inevitably overcome all obstacles because of their faith in true love and their unshakable knowledge that they belong together. This is all old hat, but what if we now tell you that the unsatisfying relationship our heroine was in before meeting the man of her dreams was a *marriage*. Suddenly, it isn't a comedy anymore. Our society will only allow the plot to move in two directions in this situation: either the movie becomes a tragedy in which the heroine leaves her marriage to discover that it wasn't true love after all, or the story ends happily when she realizes before it is too late that her husband was her true love all along.

From infancy, our children are fed true love stories, and not only in classics like "Cinderella." One of our daughters' favorite movies was called *Barbie as the Island Princess*. In this story, Barbie and her animal friends are shipwrecked on a deserted tropical island. Barbie lives there happily until a handsome prince discovers the island. He invites her back to his kingdom, and the two fall in love during the voyage home. Trouble begins when Queen Mom and King Dad disapprove of this wild girl. It turns out that the prince is already betrothed to a sweet princess named Luciana. Following a series of misunderstandings and dastardly plots, Barbie is banished from the kingdom and shipwrecked a second time. Fortunately, she is able to sneak back during the prince's wedding, disrupting the proceedings (while gratuitously saving some animals along the way) and ultimately marrying the prince.

The message to children is that true love conquers all, and that Barbie and her prince should brave all hazards and risk other relationships in their lives in order to be together. The prince risked becoming estranged from his parents by marrying Barbie, and he abandoned his bewildered fiancée at the altar. This story is considered appropriate for young children because nobody really gets hurt. It turns out that the fiancée didn't really want to marry the prince anyway, so she was happier after the breakup. The king and queen came around to accepting their new daughter-in-law, so the prince's relationship with his parents remained intact. The story is all upside and no downside, and it is gratifying to see two people so in love celebrate being together.

However, what if Barbie had been a day late getting back to the prince's kingdom? A day after the celebrant had said, "I pronounce you man and wife," the prince would have been beyond Barbie's reach. Even though the prince and princess didn't really want to be married to one another, he wouldn't have abandoned his new bride for Barbie. The moment before the wedding, the prince could kick Princess Luciana to the curb, but the moment after the wedding, that is no longer a culturally acceptable choice. Had Barbie arrived after the exchange of rings, she would have had to let go of her dream of true love. She would probably have drunk a few Shirley Temples with her animal friends, who would have told her that they never thought the prince was really all that. She would agree to a few blind dates, maybe one with a guy called Ken who would sweep her off her feet and cause her to forget all about Prince What's his name.

Meanwhile, the prince and his bride would make things work even if it wasn't true love. The prince's friends would tell him that there's no such thing as true love anyway, and he was lucky to have a bride as sweet as Princess Luciana. The same sidekicks who had egged him on to go after Barbie, throwing caution and reason to the wind, would now try to make him see that he would never have been happier with Barbie than with Luciana.

All of this makes perfect sense from the perspective of maximizing happiness without causing social upheaval. However, it can lead to a bad case of social whiplash, being told to believe in true love before marriage and then being told to let go of those aspirations if one misses finding it at the altar. It is

Udderly Personal

Before I met Celeste, I always had the feeling that there was a hole in my life. Even back when I was married for the first time, I never felt complete. Although I worked hard at a job I loved, spent happy days with my family, and had many adventures, none of these things seemed to fill that hole. I assumed that this was the human condition, and that everyone felt like I did. When I met Celeste, that hole disappeared. It was a revelation to me that so many of my efforts in life were directed at trying to fill a hole that only that kind of love could fill. Now, I am far less ambitious. I no longer need to be the best in my field or to have a life packed with adventure. If I could somehow spend every moment of the rest of my life holding Celeste in my arms, that is what I would choose.

—In Love in Los Angeles

not possible for true love to exist on one side of the moment when somebody says, "I now pronounce you man and wife," and not exist on the other side. The fact that society pushes so hard to have it both ways is a perfect example of a Sacred Cow.

Why the One True Cow is two-faced

The One True Cow wants everyone to get married and to stay married. It makes sense that she would tell married people, "You may feel like you chose the wrong mate, but there's no such thing as the 'right' person for you! True love is a myth." People are more likely to stick with an unhappy marriage if they believe that there can be no lasting romance, and if they believe that admiration and passion must inevitably die with the passage of time. Thus, if Barbie in the story above had arrived too late to halt the wedding, then the prince must be convinced that Princess Luciana will make him every bit as happy (or unhappy) as Barbie would have made him. The prince and princess are not in love, and now that they are married to one another, the One True Cow needs them both to believe that true love is a fiction. That way, they will believe that their relationship is as good as it gets, and the prince will not pine for Barbie.

That all seems logical, but why would the One True Cow want to promote the ideal of true love before marriage? Wouldn't she be more successful if she convinced everyone just to settle for Mr. or Ms. Good Enough and stop yearning for Mr. or Ms. Right?

Well, yes and no. If the One True Cow could *successfully* convince everyone to settle, then marriage rates would increase, divorce rates would decrease, and the One True Cow could contentedly retire to the pasture.

Unfortunately for this Cow, however, people are not easily convinced that they should settle for Ms. or Mr. Good Enough. In the past, people had to marry in order to have sex, have children, or to survive economically. Boredom, loneliness, and what marriage expert Stephanie Coontz calls "fond contempt" characterized many marriages up to the mid-twentieth century; pursuit of happiness was not considered a valid reason either to marry or to divorce. In the twenty-first century, however, marriage has become fully optional for many individuals in our society. Both men and women today may choose to live alone rather than risk sharing a home with someone they eventually won't love or even like.

If Barbie had believed that she would eventually find the prince uninteresting, or if she had believed that there were thousands of men out there who would make her just as happy as the prince, she might have been unwilling to take risks in order to be with him. Even if Barbie didn't have a shipwreck, the prince's fiancée, and his angry parents to deal with, the idea of marriage itself might have seemed plenty risky to her. Committing to marry takes courage, and everyone, not only Barbie, needs a lot of motivation to get over that hurdle. The cultural ideal of true love provides some of the motivation necessary to commit. Are you worried about marrying someone who is poor? "Don't worry," says the One True Cow. "You are marrying for true love, and that is much more important than money!" Are you worried that your spouse won't always love you? "Don't worry," says the One True Cow. "She is your true love, so of course she will always love you!" And so on. The One True Cow has an answer for every qualm about commitment, and her answers amount to true love being the most noble, most rewarding, and most cherished of all human aspirations.

This positive attitude towards true love serves the purposes of the One True Cow in two ways: it inspires people to get married, and once married, it inspires people to continue to feel fortunate for having found true love. A problem arises, however, when some subset of people become disillusioned with marriage. If Barbie begins to find the prince to be a poor companion, she might wonder if she did indeed marry her true love. Worse yet, if Barbie meets Ken and becomes convinced that he is in fact her true love, and that her marriage to the prince (no matter what a great guy he might be) was a tragic mistake, the One True Cow has a big problem on her hoofs. She is not going to be able to convince Barbie now that the prince is her one and only. In the first case, Barbie has already decided that if true love exists, the prince ain't it. In the second case, Barbie has already fallen in love, and the One True Cow won't be able to convince Barbie that what she felt for the prince was true love, whereas what she feels for Ken is some poor facsimile. At this point, the One True Cow has no choice but to tell Barbie that true love does not exist.

The One True Cow will tell Barbie that true love is a cruel Hollywood invention with the sole purpose of selling movies. She will tell her that her unhappiness with the prince can be fixed by a visit to the Expert Cow, and that her marriage is as good as any marriage could be. The One True Cow will sigh and tut-tut when Barbie confesses her feelings for Ken, saying things like, "You don't know what it's like to be married to Ken," and, "Your feelings for Ken will disappear faster than a snowball in June." The One True Cow will erode Barbie's belief in true love,

The late screenwriter Nora Ephron was a guest on the NPR program *Wait Wait… Don't Tell Me*. The host (Peter Sagal) asked her, "You have made some of the most successful romantic comedies of all time where everybody is charming and funny and self-aware and it all ends up great in the end … Are you trying to ruin it for everybody?" (Brave question from someone whose wife may be listening.)

NE: "Isn't your life like that?"
PS: "Not yet."
NE: "No? Are you married or divorced?"
PS: "I'm in fact married."
NE: "You are? Well … What are you complaining about?"

It seems from this exchange that the only thing you can complain about is not being married. This is from the twice-divorced writer of some of our favorite stories of true love!

undoing the Cow's own previous work. She will know that she has succeeded if Barbie accepts that the feelings she wishes that she had in her marriage (or thought that she had for Ken) are an unattainable dream.

Love is a four-letter word

You don't hear much about love in marriage self-help books, let alone true love. In fact, the word "love" almost never appears but is referred to in amusingly euphemistic ways. In his book *The Seven Principles for Making Marriage Work*, John Gottman states, "… happy marriages are based on a deep friendship. By this I mean a mutual respect for and enjoyment of each other's company. These couples tend to know each other intimately— they are well versed in each other's likes, dislikes, personality quirks, hopes and dreams. They have an abiding regard for each other and express this fondness not just in the big ways but in little ways day in and day out." This is a fair—if long-winded— description of what most of us would simply call "love." Why do Gottman and others so studiously avoid what seems to most of us an innocuous word?

We speculate that the reason why authors of self-help books rarely mention "love" is that they don't have suggestions for how to create love. There is no "love" switch that you can turn on inside your heart to awaken a feeling that most of us can't even describe. If such a switch existed, lonely singles could ask dating sites to identify compatible marriage partners and then simply flip on their love switches. It would be happily ever after for the couples and 100% success rate for eHarmony. Unfortunately, people can no more force themselves to be in love than they can force themselves to believe in leprechauns. True love, in particular, is so tied to the identity of the love object that, by definition, it can't be felt for just anybody—possibly not even for the person one happens to have married. Self-help books for couples in trouble are supposed to offer action items, and so the books focus on things like intimacy and respect that can be practiced and possibly improved.

Whether intimacy and respect are viable substitutes for love is a highly subjective question. There is a concept in the art world that craftsmanship is not art, and though art is impossible to define, nothing else is an acceptable substitute. Similarly, while we cannot properly define true love, many of us have the sense that there is not an acceptable substitute. Since we can't spend our lives wandering the world in search of our other halves, however, we buy self-help books in the hope that cultivation of intimacy and respect will trigger the secret switch inside our hearts.

A further irony found in the Gottman quotation above is that he seems to be saying, "Happy marriages require love." If happy marriages require love, and if love cannot be conjured at will, then it seems appropriate to admit that not all marriages can or should be saved. This admission does not sell books, however, which is another reason why "love" is a four-letter word in the world of marital self-help.

> Getting divorced just because you don't love a man is almost as silly as getting married just because you do.
> —Zsa Zsa Gabor

Brenda & George

George was a quiet, studious graduate student when he met Brenda, a vivacious extrovert. After a year of dating, Brenda suggested that they get married, and George bought her a ring. They enjoyed financial success and had two healthy children, and both George and Brenda would have described themselves as happy if anyone had asked. They grew progressively more distant from one another, however, and Brenda would complain that George never spontaneously demonstrated physical affection. George would make an effort for a day or two before relapsing back to his old habits. Brenda suggested that they see a marriage counselor, but George refused, saying that "Marriage counselors are for couples who fight and have problems, but we don't have any problems." The years went by, with Brenda and George living separate lives under the same roof. Eventually, Brenda found herself attracted to another man, and she told George that she wanted out of the marriage. George responded that he wanted to save their marriage, and he begged Brenda to work with him to rekindle their love.

Brenda respects and cares for George as a friend, but all feelings of romantic love have died over the years. At this point, the couple has three choices: They can hope that Brenda's love for George is not extinguished but simply buried under layers of unconscious grievances, and they can work to remove those grievances. Alternatively, George can try to convince Brenda that the kind of "love" Brenda thinks is missing is only a myth. Third, they could acknowledge that Brenda no longer loves George (and perhaps George no longer loves Brenda) and begin to sort out whether or how they could stay married under those circumstances.

The first of these options would presumably be the best for everybody if it could work. The family would remain intact, Brenda and George would both be happier, and the One True Cow would leave them alone. The One True Cow would only step in if it started to look as though love might not be recoverable. In that case, she would either try to stall indefinitely on option one, telling George and Brenda that love is surely about to return any second now, or she would skip to option two, her old standby.

Interestingly, what the One True Cow would never do is encourage option three (where Brenda and George acknowledge that the love is gone and figure out what to do about it). She knows that it is untenable in the twenty-first century to expect loveless couples to stay married if they believe in true love. The One True Cow is cynical about true love, and she has little patience for Plato and his theories about humans having two halves. However, she understands that Plato was onto something when he spoke of human longing for love. Plato wrote, "Love is born into every human being; it calls back the halves of our original nature together; it tries to make one out of two and heal the wounds of human nature." The longing for love will keep happily married couples together, but it will drive unhappily married couples apart. This is why the One True Cow has only two options for married couples: they must be in love, or they must believe that true love does not exist. There is no third option for the One True Cow.

True love and white weddings

It is traditional in Western culture for brides to wear white. Originally a sign of conspicuous consumption (because white is so darned difficult to clean), the white dress came to symbolize the bride's innocence and sexual purity. Although our society no longer expects women to marry young or to remain virginal until their wedding nights, the tradition of the white dress remains strong. Strong, that is, for first weddings. A different expectation exists when it comes to second weddings.

Etiquette websites are full of suggestions about how second-time brides can tastefully navigate the tricky dress color choice. Since the second-time bride presumably has not slipped further down some virginity scale since her first wedding, the problem with white can't be a lack of sexual purity. While nobody can say for certain why white is popular for first weddings and not for second weddings, we propose the hypothesis that the symbolic power of white has become attached to our cultural narrative of true love rather than to virginity. Our culture allows (and even expects) that the bride is in the throes of true love on her first wedding day. The definitional fact that you can't have true love with more than one person in the same lifetime means that she cannot have true love on her second wedding day. Or anyway, she admitted by getting a divorce that it wasn't true love the first time around, and she is a fool if she doesn't go into her second marriage with a generous helping of cynicism.

The One True Cow approves of this attitude. She does not want second marriages to be as romantic as first marriages, because she fears that will erode the stigma of divorce. As a society, we have let go of the belief that good girls don't have sex, and we expect first-time brides with well-filled little black books to wear white without a shred of irony. One day, maybe our society will admit that who you marry first and true love do not, sadly, always coincide, and allow for the same expressions of hope and joy at second weddings as at first.

Conclusion

Whether you are an apostle or an apostate of true love, we hope that this chapter has revealed to you the hypocrisy of the One True Cow. She deserves her rank among the Sacred Cows not because of her beliefs with respect to true love, but because she cynically promotes opposite views in order to achieve her ends. She will sing the praises of love if that will encourage marriage, but she will take it all back again if that will discourage divorce. This hypocrisy can only lead to confusion, which is not a state that promotes sound decision making. Let's send this Cow back to the barn!

CHAPTER SEVEN
The Other Cow

Adultery—which is the only grounds for divorce in
New York—is not grounds for divorce in California.
As a matter of fact, adultery in Southern California
is grounds for marriage.
—Allan Sherman

Meet the Cow

The Other Cow is an easily titillated Cow that feeds on jealousy and gossip. She may come across as an idle busybody, but she has an agenda—to make it socially unacceptable for anyone to divorce in order to marry a new person. She is the most judgmental of the Cows and the most spiteful. Guilt and shame are her preferred tools.

Caveat: Tipping over the Other Cow is not a defense of piggishness or deception. This Cow only insists that it is always wrong to leave a marriage to be with a new person.

The sixth commandment

The tragedy began with Tristan and Iseult, but it certainly didn't end there. Dante reserved a special circle of hell for adulterers, and Anna Karenina ended up under the wheels of a train after she cheated on her husband. Hester Prynne was famously banished from society for the same sin. Moses brought the sixth commandment down from Mount Sinai, and the Torah prescribes the death penalty for adultery. There is little question about where Western culture stands on the issue of adultery, and probably with good reason. Families can be fragmented and hearts broken when a spouse strays. It can be destabilizing for any society to have a bunch of married people stepping out, and so we have developed social pressures to discourage such activities. Yet disapproval meted out by our society does not seem sufficient to stop adultery. Though reports vary widely, a significant number of married individuals in America are currently engaged in an extramarital affair, and not surprisingly, infidelity is commonly cited as a contributing factor in divorce.[1]

Although adultery is a fascinating subject, as magazines in grocery checkout lines make clear, this chapter is not really about people cheating on their spouses. The Sacred Cow in this case is not the commandment "You shouldn't have affairs," but rather the cultural assumption that "You are a bad person because you want to leave your marriage to be with someone else." However, anyone leaving a marriage for another person must have had some type of pre-divorce extramarital relationship, so let's start by looking at how often this occurs.

It turns out to be a little difficult to pin down exactly how common extramarital affairs are in American society. The answer depends upon how we define "extramarital affair," which population we ask, and how carefully we gather the information. As you might imagine, not everyone is willing to be *totally* honest with a researcher on this topic, and what some people call an "affair," others might call "a little innocent flirtation" or "a close friendship." Also, some people don't count sex acts other than intercourse in the category of "sexual relations" (See

"Monicagate," "Lewinskygate," Bill Clinton, 1998).

In large national samples of heterosexual couples, the number of people reporting that they have had extramarital sexual intercourse is in the range of 10-25%.[2-5] Some researchers, such as the infidelity expert Shirley Glass, have reported numbers as high as 25% for wives and 44% for husbands.[6] If the definition of "affair" is expanded to include romantic or sexual relationships that do not involve sexual intercourse, then numbers up to 50% have been reported. That seems like an extremely high number, but we have to wonder what those numbers really mean as the definition of "affair" becomes increasingly broad and subjective. (You might think that the dinners with your colleague are innocent kvetching sessions about office politics, while your co-worker might think it's true love.) However, if we believe the data that use the stricter definition of affairs as involving sexual intercourse, we could conservatively conclude that extramarital affairs occur in approximately one-fifth to one-quarter of married, heterosexual relationships in the United States.

Since our Other Cow is targeting the subset of people who leave their spouses for an affair partner, we should ask how many of these affairs result in divorce. Although that number is not known with certainty, it is estimated that in approximately one-third of divorces, one or both spouses had been romantically involved with another person before the marriage fell apart.[7] Some studies have found, not surprisingly, that affairs are the single strongest corollary of divorce.[8]

If we put all of this together, what we can say with some degree of certainty is that extramarital affairs are common, that many people who have affairs don't divorce, but that affairs and divorce go together like peanut butter and jelly. Of course the fact those two things (affairs and divorce) go together does not tell us anything about causation. Chest pain and heart attacks are strongly associated, but it is not safe to say that chest pain causes heart attacks. Similarly, affairs may cause divorce, or unhappy marriages may cause both affairs and divorce independently.

In either event, affairs can be one of the most complicated, painful parts of divorce. Betrayed partners are burdened with feelings of bitterness and injustice beyond what they might otherwise have experienced in divorce, and betrayers are frequently beset by guilt. Affairs provide a convenient stick with which family and friends can beat cheaters about the head and shoulders, sometimes in hope of forestalling divorce. The social stigma of adultery makes it easy to label one spouse as a victim and the other as a villain, which provides fertile fields for Sacred Cows to inhabit and exploit.

> I don't think I'll get married again. I'll just find a woman I don't like and give her a house.
>
> —Lewis Grizzard

A thought experiment: How much do you agree with this Sacred Cow?

Most people would agree that adultery is bad. Adultery almost inevitably involves deception and betrayal, and even if you think that divorce is sometimes okay, you are unlikely to agree that it is acceptable to unilaterally break your marriage vows without even having the decency to inform your spouse.

On the other hand, if you think that divorce is sometimes acceptable, you are unlikely to have a strong opinion about whether or not it is okay for people to get married a second time. The idea that a divorced person can remarry is not offensive to most people in our society.

It may not seem obvious at first, but between remarriage (acceptable to most of us) and adultery (unacceptable to most of us) lays a long continuum. The continuum consists of the time when the new partner appears relative to the end of the marriage. If partner #2 shows up while the marriage is intact, we call it adultery. If partner #2 shows up years after divorce, we call it remarriage. If partner #2 shows up while the marriage is on the rocks but before the divorce decree is signed, well, it's not clear what to call it, other than an uncomfortable situation.

The Other Cow, like all Sacred Cows, opposes anybody

getting divorced. She therefore exploits our society's negative feelings about adultery to pressure people into staying married. She knows that when a couple goes public about their split, the existence of partner #2 will be revealed, inciting gossip and social disapproval. This is a disincentive to separating (and also, ironically, an incentive to lie about partner #2). In order to illustrate how the Other Cow uses blurry moral lines to discourage divorce, consider this hypothetical situation:

Imagine that you have a friend named Jose who is considering leaving his marriage. You are aware that Jose has been chronically unhappy, though he has never told you that his marriage is absolutely unbearable. Jose has shared his many troubles with you over the years, and you have witnessed the failure of every effort to improve the marriage. One day, Jose tells you that he wants to ask his wife for a divorce, because he has become convinced that he and his wife are fundamentally incompatible. He hopes to someday find the right person with whom to share his life, and he does not want to waste another year in his current state of loneliness and unhappiness. Jose asks whether you agree that his decision to divorce is reasonable.

We know that the Other Cow would say, "No way, Jose!" The Other Cow believes that nobody should leave a marriage in hope of building a better marriage with someone else. Do you agree with her? If you do, you might tell Jose that the grass is never truly greener on the other side, and that there is no such thing as being married to the "right" or "wrong" person. Alternatively, you might agree with the Other Cow not because you believe divorce itself to be immoral, but because you believe that leaving to be with someone else is immoral, even if that person is abstract.

For those of you who would have let Jose out of his marriage, let's change a few things. Imagine that unhappy Jose could not bring himself to ask for a divorce, until one day he saw the woman of his dreams at a coffee shop. You need to suspend your disbelief for this part of the thought experiment, and imagine that we live in an alternate universe where people can tell at a glance whether they are truly made for one another.

Through magic, Jose knew instantly that the woman he saw in the coffee shop was his soul mate, though they never exchanged a word. Jose does not know whether this woman is single, whether she is straight, or whether he will ever find her again. Jose tells you that just knowing for certain that this woman exists has made him realize that he cannot stay married to his wife. He understands that his marriage is worse than the poor compromise he had always believed it to be; he now sees his marriage as a lie. He asks you whether you support his decision to ask his wife for a divorce.

If you now join the Cow at this point in saying, "No way, Jose!" that tells you something interesting about your psyche. You were willing to support Jose leaving his marriage for the abstract chance of a better relationship, but now that there is a concrete "other woman" involved, it presumably makes you feel squeamish. Perhaps you feel that it is more unfair or cruel for Jose to leave his wife for another woman rather than for the abstract possibility of a better life.

If you still think that Jose is not being unreasonable or immoral, here is the next question. Let's say that Jose didn't have the magical ability to tell that the woman in the coffee shop was his true love, but he spent many hours with her in increasingly intense but platonic encounters until he fell deeply in love. He becomes convinced that staying married to his wife would not only be hypocritical but absolutely unbearable now that he has discovered this new depth of feeling for someone else. Jose asks whether you believe him to be a bad person because he feels that he must divorce his wife.

Many of us would start siding with the Other Cow right about now, probably at least in part because we do not want our spouses getting to know people in coffee shops too intimately. It is a strange time to start agreeing with the Other Cow, though, when you think about it. What we are saying if we wag our fingers at Jose here is that it's okay for him to get divorced with the remote hope of marrying someone he truly loves, but it's not okay to become acquainted with that person before he gets divorced. It is as though the low probability of Jose finding the woman of his dreams gives him moral cover. If Jose is unlikely to ever find the coffee shop woman again, then it's okay to get divorced. If he's likely to start dating the coffee shop woman as soon as he separates from his wife, though, that's not okay. Ask yourself this: If you happened to know that the coffee shop woman will reject Jose's advances, would that change how you feel about whether he should stay with his wife?

For those who have so far refrained from finger wagging, please consider the final installment of this thought experiment. Jose and the coffee shop woman have talked over many a latte, and they are absolutely convinced that they are meant to be together. Clear in that knowledge, they arrange to meet privately and have romantic physical contact for the first time. Maybe angels sing and maybe not, but in any case, Jose tells you that he can no longer pretend to himself that he isn't having an affair. He recognizes that he has to come clean to his wife and ask her for a divorce, and he regrets having been too chicken to do this earlier. He wonders whether he caused the relationship to become sexual because he was trying to force his own hand. Jose worries that he is a bad person and asks whether you agree.

For those of you who are only now changing your minds about the moral nature of Jose's choices, it is interesting to note that you had already given Jose a free pass to fall in love with this woman. The hotel room was an awfully late addition to the relationship for it to be the sole focus of moral qualms. More importantly, if you now agree that Jose has done a bad thing, does that make him a bad person for getting divorced? The Other Cow wants you to extend your negative feelings about extramarital sex to divorce, so that your disapproval for one will change your advice to Jose on the other.

If Jose could somehow go back in time to the year before he met the coffee shop woman, he could divorce his wife without interference from the Other Cow. He might have to contend with other Sacred Cows, but this particular piece of social condemnation would be removed. As it is, he can either proceed with telling his wife that he wants out of the marriage, knowing that he will receive harsh judgment, or he can cover up the affair.

(He could also confess the affair and try to rebuild his marriage, but this thought experiment is about someone who no longer wants to be married.) Which course of action do you advise?

This thought experiment was designed to test your feeling about whether people can leave marriage to be with someone else without being morally bankrupt. By separating the issue of divorce from the issue of extramarital sex by several steps, we hope that you have been able to better pinpoint what makes you morally uncomfortable and what doesn't. If you found yourself saying, "No way, Jose!" from the very beginning, then you may not even accept that the Other Cow belongs among the Sacred Cows. However, if you made it at least part way through the exercise thinking that Jose was reasonable, then you have begun to see for yourself what this Other Cow can look like.

Udderly Personal

Like a lot of people, I sometimes wonder what I would do if my husband cheated on me. I see it like this: If Robert told me that he was having an affair and was in love with this other woman, I would be totally devastated. I would be furious, emotionally shattered and frightened of starting my life over at my age. If I had the option of scraping the tatters of my life together and starting over alone or clinging to Robert, knowing that he doesn't love me, which would make me happier? Obviously the first choice: Either outcome is terrible, but it would be worse to live with a caged beast who was a constant emotional drag on my life.

On the other hand, if Robert confessed the affair and begged my forgiveness, telling me that he still loved me more than anyone else, would I stay? Yes, I would stay, but not for noble reasons. Not because I value the commitment (that he has already broken). I would stay for purely selfish reasons, because as long as he still loves me, I would rather be with him than apart from him almost no matter how badly he behaves. I think this is what makes the difference between staying and leaving: Love.

—Wondering in Walla Walla

Walk a mile in Anna Karenina's shoes

Anna Karenina is perhaps the most famous cautionary tale about adultery ever written. After abandoning her husband for her lover, Anna becomes entirely socially isolated and consumed with misery over losing her son. At one point in the story, Anna says to a visitor, Levin, "Please tell your wife that I'm just as fond of her as ever and that if she can not forgive me my situation I don't want her ever to forgive me. To forgive she would have to live through what I have lived through and may God preserve her from that." Anna knows that Levin's wife Kitty may be angry or disgusted with her, and that those feelings can preclude sympathy. She believes that Kitty could not understand her without experiencing the same pain that she is suffering. Tolstoy allows the reader to witness Anna's passion, as well as her humiliation and agony, and by the time she throws herself under a train at the end of the book, the reader has a softer view of Anna's transgressions than Kitty might have had.

Anna Karenina is a powerful example of how context and empathy can affect social attitudes towards infidelity. Our society is motivated to judge adulterers harshly, but we also feel compassion for our unfaithful friends and family members when we can understand the reasons for their choices. These conflicting feelings sometimes lead to unconscious hypocrisy in how we treat adulterers, offering sympathy to those we love and judgment against those we don't love. Below, we present an illustration of this unconscious double standard, as well as examples of how society's disapproval of infidelity can be used as a tool to discourage divorce.

The letter

Once family and friends discover an affair, at least one lecture is bound to arrive in the mail or in-box of the betrayer. It usually comes from a person who is more invested in the continuation of the marriage than in the personal happiness of the adulterer.

Dear Ann,

I was shocked and saddened to hear the news that you and Jeff are going through such a hard time. Sarah and I have always seen you two as the perfect couple—so I'm sure you two will find a way through this together. I hope that you know that we are both here for you, and not just for Jeff. As your husband's best friend, I can assure you that he dotes on you. I hope you have not forgotten how lucky you are to be with a great guy like Jeff. When Jeff told me what was going on, my initial reaction was (yes) one of censure: "What?! What the h … is she thinking? Spiritual connection? Soul mate? Excuse me, but that's b … s …"

Let me tell you a story. My parents have been happily married for 45 years, but when I was a little kid, my parents went through a rough patch like you and Jeff are having right now. My mother seriously thought about leaving my father. But she didn't. She stuck it out and they did the hard work and now she says, "Thank god I didn't leave." My mother's friend, on the other hand, went through something similar at about the same time, and she did leave. She is still married to her second husband, but it's a lot of hard work, and it's made harder by the baggage she brought to her second marriage. Once she was faced with all of the mundane aspects of life in her new marriage, like doing dishes and paying the mortgage, she saw that her new husband wasn't so perfect after all. She realizes that if she had just done the hard work with her first husband, she would be better off now.

Incidentally, I too have had the spiritual/true love feeling while in another relationship (much to my chagrin now). I had been dating a wonderful woman when I met a woman in Peru who floored me completely and captured my heart. When I broke up with my girlfriend, I sincerely used the "soul mate" line, and she replied, "But that's what I thought we had." I took a six-month sabbatical to live with Woman #2, and she broke up with me the week I arrived. Why am I sharing this? I don't know. It's the first thing I thought of when I heard the words "spiritual connection." I guess my point is that those feelings can change.

I know I would not be the person I am today if it weren't for my relationship with Sarah. It's not perfect by any means, and I know that there are other people in the world who would have been a good match and led me in a different direction. It's definitely a challenge to maintain the passion, and I think we could do better on that front. My hope is that through a long period of sharing, supporting, and yes, sometimes sacrificing for each other (Sarah doesn't like when I talk like this!) we can develop a very strong foundation. It's a lot to ask of another person for sure, but I think it's true what the Bible says too: you reap what you sow.

Perhaps it's appropriate to remember the quote from Rilke that I read at your wedding (this is not meant to be a guilt trip in any way!!!). "For one human being to love another: that is perhaps the most difficult of all our tasks, the ultimate, the last test and proof, the work for which all other work is but preparation." To that, we can now say, AMEN! You are in that "ultimate" place right now.

I know that you are feeling lost and confused, and it will be very hard for you to dig yourself out of the hole you have created. You will have to work incredibly hard to try to regain Jeff's trust and to get your marriage back on solid footing. I hope some of these thoughts can be useful to you on the long journey back toward a happy marriage with Jeff. If I can help you along that path, all you need to do is ask.

With love,

Arnold

This letter illustrates several themes in the advice given by well-meaning friends and family when someone they know strays from marriage and considers divorce. The Other Cow (who believes that it is never okay to leave a marriage in order to be with a different partner) shows up in a number of ways we will describe below. You will also spot some of the other Sacred Cows in Arnold's letter if you keep a keen lookout:

The grass is always greener (because you don't have to mow it): People leaving one relationship for another will often be told that the grass won't look so green once they get to the other side of the fence. As Arnold implies in the story about his mother's friend, once you begin to truly share your life with someone, the romance gets lost in fights over taking out the garbage or putting down the toilet seat. In other words, once you start having to mow that greener grass, it looks about the same shade of green as the grass you were used to looking at before. The logical fallacy of this argument is that grass does in fact come in different shades of green. Not all marriages are created equal; if they were, people wouldn't put so much energy into dating. People care a great deal about choosing the right person to marry, and it doesn't make a lot of sense to say, "It doesn't matter who you chose; any Tom, Dick or Harry would make you just as happy/unhappy." Unless Ann lives on a golf green, presumably greener grass exists for her *somewhere* in the world. It is true that people who are unhappy with their current circumstance are vulnerable to seeing other circumstances as superior, and those new circumstances certainly don't always turn out to be better. It is irrational, however, to state that circumstances *never* turn out to be better. Besides, green is in the eye of the beholder, and Arnold does not know what will make Ann happiest.

The toothpaste test: Some people call a variant of the "green grass" platitude the "toothpaste test" in honor of the timeworn argument between spouses about putting the cap on the toothpaste or squeezing from the bottom. Here is how the toothpaste test works: When someone like Ann is considering leaving her marriage for someone else, a friend like Arnold will say, "You have no idea what irritating habits your new beau might have until you live with him. He seems great now, but imagine how you will feel when you have to wipe up the toothpaste from the counter every night." This is essentially a "better the devil you know than the devil you don't" argument. This argument has some merit, but the clue to holes in its logic is that the attitude is not applied consistently. When Ann was single and considering marrying Jeff, Arnold wasn't saying, "Whoa there, Ann, you'd better think twice about whether you want to marry this guy when you have no idea how he handles tubes of toothpaste. In fact, I can tell you from having lived with him at Kappa Omicron Omega Sigma (KOWS) that he makes an ungodly mess in the bathroom."

Love is fickle: Arnold is too gracious to say this in his letter, but the story about his own misguided pursuit of his soul mate touches on this theme. Arnold gave up a relationship for someone he felt passionately about, and then he was himself abandoned. He is warning Ann not only that true love is merely an illusion (see the One True Cow chapter), but that the object of her love may decide at any moment that he does not want to be with her after all. This is, of course, an entirely reasonable warning. That said, given the significant prevalence of divorce and of infidelity in marriages, Arnold could just as reasonably have warned Ann to beware of Jeff (or Jeff to beware of Ann) when they got married.

Leaving marriage is taking the easy road: Arnold dwells on the need for hard work and sacrifice to keep marriage intact. He is not just extolling the virtue of hard work; he is implying that choosing to end a marriage is the lazy thing to do. He also states that second marriages require even more sacrifice and hard work than first marriages; presumably he means this as a deterrent for Ann. Arnold can't logically have it both ways, however. Either hard work is something we should all try to avoid, in which case Ann would be better off single, if being single is so easy. Or, if the hard work of marriage is a virtue, then Ann should seek out as much marriage and hard work as she can by taking on that second marriage.

I know that your spouse is the best choice for you: Arnold is so busy praising Jeff that he leaves no room for how Jeff actually makes Ann feel. This is insulting to Ann, since Arnold can't possibly know how happy Ann has been with Jeff, nor how happy she could be in an alternate relationship. Arnold sincerely believes that Jeff is a good guy, and he is trying to be a good friend to Jeff by helping him to preserve his marriage. Arnold isn't terribly concerned about Ann's happiness, however, and he is using Ann's guilt as a tool to help Jeff, not to help Ann.

The partner who had the affair is solely responsible for the failure of the marriage: The subtext of Arnold's letter is that Ann is the bad guy. He tells her that she needs to dig herself out of the hole that *she* created, and that she is responsible for doing the hard work required to get the marriage back on solid footing. Most people, when talking abstractly about relationships, would agree that it "takes two to tango." If it's true in the abstract that the health of any relationship is the responsibility of both parties, then how a relationship ends should not suddenly alter this reality. It is possible that Jeff was a perfect husband for Ann until the day that she told him that she was in love with somebody else. It is certainly true that Ann has broken her wedding vow by falling in love with another man, whether or not the relationship is sexual. However, Arnold should at least consider the possibility that Ann and Jeff's marriage was unhappy for reasons that were both of their faults or nobody's fault.

I really care about you too: Arnold says to Ann, "I hope that you know that we are both here for *you*, and not just for Jeff." One time out of ten (that is a made-up statistic with no primary source reference just like the ones you'll find in relationship self-help books; we are just giving our opinion here), the Arnolds of the world really will be there for the Anns of the world, no matter what life path Ann chooses to follow. Nine times out of ten, that's not what happens. If Ann decides to leave her marriage, chances are very good that she will never hear from Arnold again. Arnold may not be aware that he is doing this, but he is offering her the warmth she desperately needs so that she will be open to his suggestions and comments in the rest of the letter. A different interpretation of Arnold's pseudo-caring is that he is hedging his relationship bets. If he is too rude or mean to Ann, then if Jeff and Ann reconcile, Arnold will not be invited back for Thanksgiving dinner.

It may seem like we're being a bit hard on Arnold in the interpretation of his letter. The truth, though, is that he is a hypocrite. To some degree, we are all hypocrites, in that we hold the people we love to different standards than everybody else. In this particular case, Arnold is taking moral potshots at Ann that he would not take if the situation were different. What kind of a letter do you think Arnold would have written if it were Jeff, his best friend, who was having the affair and thinking of leaving the marriage? Let's read it and see how emotional context can change our moral compasses.

> *Jeff,*
>
> *I'm not sure where to start. First, I guess, I'm really honored that you would share these feelings with me and I want you to know that I'm there for you. I can only imagine what you're going through.*
>
> *I always liked Ann a lot and thought you two had it all— but I can also see how perhaps there was a lot going on behind the scenes. Sarah and I have our problems too. I mostly keep that sort of stuff private, but I've told you in the past about some of it and, to be completely honest, there have definitely been weeks when staying with her seemed like the wrong choice.*
>
> *Believe me, Jeff, I get it. Ann will freak. Then Ann will tell her family and some of your close friends, and they will come down on you like a ton of bricks. They'll lecture you about the grass never really being greener and all that. And of course*

it often isn't, which you know perfectly well. But in this case, who knows? Who are they (or me) to judge whether you and Abby are soul mates or not? (Though from your description she sounds beyond amazing.) You may be this crazy about her still in a year or a decade, or not. But only you have any chance of predicting that outcome correctly. Or predicting whether you and Ann can get back to a place where you're passionate about your marriage again.

I know you, Jeff. You're a fighter. If there was any way you saw to make your marriage with Ann great again, I know you'd still be relentlessly pursuing it. If you decide to stay in your marriage, everyone will say that you'll never be able to make it up to Ann for what you've done. I'm not saying that having an affair is okay. It's not good, obviously. You know that. But it takes two to tango, as they say. Don't forget that. Making the marriage work isn't your job by yourself. If it isn't working, that is 50% your fault and 50% her fault. Just because you're the one saying things are broken doesn't change the fact that a couple has joint responsibility for making a relationship work.

Ugh. I'm starting to lecture you. I'm sorry, Jeff. I want so much to help you. I can hear how upset you are by all of this. Seriously, if there is anything I can do for you, you name it, right?

Obviously I won't talk about this to anyone. Please do let me know when you talk to Ann. If I have to take sides, though I'd rather not, I'll obviously pick you. But until you talk to her, I want to make sure to not seem weird to her.

Good luck with everything, my man. Remember, no one but you can figure out what is the right thing to do.

Big hugs, brother.
Arnold

This is the same Arnold, writing to the same Jeff about the same Ann. He is a nice, sincere guy who cares about Jeff and probably likes Ann too. It is natural for him to be more supportive of his friend than of his friend's wife; that's not a Sacred Cow. The Sacred Cow is not that he treats them differently, but that he holds Ann to a much different standard while encouraging her to recommit to Jeff. Arnold tells Ann that it's a mistake to leave, that she is the bad guy, and that she needs to do the hard work to get the marriage back on track. He tells Jeff that it's understandable to leave, that he's not a bad guy, and that the marital problems are probably half Ann's fault. When he writes to Ann, Arnold is channeling the Other Cow, who uses every argument she can muster to keep unfaithful spouses from initiating divorce. When Arnold writes to Jeff, he is just trying to be a good friend. The daylight we can see between Arnold's two letters is, as much as anything, a measure of the size of this Sacred Cow.

The Bad News Bears of marriage

One of the statistics you will hear bandied about is that second marriages fail at an even higher rate than first marriages. The implication is that you will be even more unhappy in your second marriage than your first, so you had better not leave your first spouse for anyone else. The best data we could find about rates of divorce of first and second marriages bear out the claim that second marriages are less likely to last than first marriages. Our data come from a 2001 CDC report entitled "First Marriage Dissolution, Divorce, and Remarriage: United States," by Bramlett and Mosher. This report presents national estimates of the duration of first and second marriages for women, though data for second marriages covers only ten years. According to this study, 20% of first marriages end by 5 years compared with 23% of second marriages, and 33% of first marriages end by 10 years compared with 39% of second marriages. So from these data, we can conclude that the divorce rate is at least 3-6% higher for second marriages than for first marriages. That difference may not be big enough for people to plan their lives around, but let's conduct a thought experiment about these statistics.

Let's pretend that people in their first and second marriages are on two different sports teams, and they are competing to see who will have the lowest divorce rate. The "first marriage" team is somewhat disadvantaged by having players who are teenagers (youths are statistically likely to divorce), but these represent a miniscule percentage of their players. The "first marriage" team also has a huge number of players who for religious, ethical or social reasons refuse to divorce no matter how unhappy their marriages. On the other hand, the "second marriage" team has players with a proven willingness to accept divorce as a solution to marital unhappiness. They also have players whose marriages ended in the context of mental illness or substance dependency, or who are otherwise temperamentally unsuited for marriage. Many couples in the second marriage team are burdened by the stress of ex-spouses, stepchildren and all of the complications of family blending. The "second marriage" team are the Bad

Udderly Personal

When I found out that my husband was having an affair, I was completely devastated. Although we had had our problems, I still loved him deeply and wanted to stay married to him. He seemed to feel terrible about what he had done, and he agreed to do everything he could to patch things up. I thought that we were doing okay, but a few years later he had another affair. We went through the same process the second time around, but things never really got back to happy. We tried everything … counseling, retreats, vacations. Nothing seemed to lift us out of the devastation this time. Finally, a friend said to me, "You know, if he's having affairs, that means that he's just not that into you." It was an epiphany for me. He kept saying that he loved me and that he wanted to fix our marriage, but of course he really wasn't into me anymore. He didn't love me the way I loved him or the way I deserved to be loved. That was when I realized that we had to divorce. I miss him sometimes, and we have become good friends, but I am much happier now. When I look back, I can see how many years of unnecessary heartache I went through because I blinded myself to the simple fact that my husband didn't love me anymore.

—Recovering in Reno

News Bears of the divorce competition. They don't stand a chance of having a lower divorce rate than the "first marriage" team. Yet even so, they lose by only a few percentage points. Do the statistics really indicate that second marriages are doomed, or do they in fact suggest that quite a few people are happier with their second spouses? We leave it for you to be the umpire on this decision.

Are we hypocrites when it comes to affairs?

We started this chapter by talking about the harsh attitudes of Western culture toward affairs. We then went on to describe the surprisingly large number of Americans who cop to having had extramarital affairs, which at least suggests an element of hypocrisy. We think that another form of hypocrisy can be found in one of the basic formulas for American romantic comedies.

As an example, let's look at the popular movie *Sleepless in Seattle*. In this story, Annie is engaged to a sweet, gentle, thoughtful man named Walter. She claims that she is "madly in love" with him. But when she hears the widowed architect Sam on the radio describing how much he misses his deceased wife, she is deeply moved and becomes obsessed with meeting Sam.

Annie writes a letter to Sam, asking him to meet her at the top of the Empire State Building on Valentine's Day (which happens to be the same day she has promised to have a romantic dinner at the Rainbow Room with her fiancé, Walter). Annie also lies to Walter when she fabricates an excuse to fly to Seattle to meet Sam. Ultimately, when Annie decides that she needs to call off her engagement, the most mature lines in the movie are given to the jilted Walter: "Look, Annie, I love you. But let's leave that out of this. I don't want to be someone that you're settling for. I don't want to be someone that anyone settles for. Marriage is hard enough without bringing such low expectations into it. Isn't it?"

Sleepless in Seattle is considered to be one of the most

romantic of all modern movies, even though it is essentially about someone having an affair. It is interesting to imagine what the movie would look like if Walter and Annie were actually married instead of engaged. What if Annie had heard Sam's voice on the radio the week after her wedding? Would she magically have been uninterested in Sam once she was wearing her wedding ring instead of her engagement ring? Or would she still have pursued Sam and told Walter that she wanted a divorce? Suddenly, it doesn't sound romantic or funny anymore.

Part of what makes *Sleepless in Seattle* romantic is that meeting Sam saves Annie from marrying the wrong guy. Walter is an okay guy, but it is clear in retrospect that Annie and Sam have much more chemistry than Annie and Walter. The audience cheers Annie on because nobody wants to see her make the mistake of settling for Walter. Even Walter acknowledges that the marriage would have been a mistake, and the audience understands that it was a very near miss indeed. Yet if Annie had met Sam after her wedding to Walter, would anyone agree with Annie that she had made a mistake? There is a Sacred Cow lurking here.

The Other Cow finds her opening because although most Americans recognize personal happiness as a valid reason for ending a relationship, few people would actively support Annie leaving her marriage for Sam. It is clear to the movie audience that Annie would be far happier with Sam than with Walter, but if Annie met Sam after marrying Walter, the audience wouldn't want her to get divorced. This situation would not invite Sacred Cows if society were willing to be open with Annie about its motives. However, the Other Cow barges right in because we fail to be honest. If we were being honest with Annie, we would throw our collective societal arm over her shoulder and say, "Look, hon, we know that you are heartbroken and that you believe you made a mistake by marrying Walter before you met Sam. You may have lifelong regrets, and you may resent Walter for keeping you from the relationship you believe is right for you. We really want you to stay married to Walter for our sake, though, and we appreciate your self-sacrifice."

Instead of this, we collectively tell Annie that she wouldn't actually be happier with Sam, and that she is being foolish to consider leaving her marriage. We tell her that the grass isn't really greener, that all marriages are equal, and that Sam probably doesn't know how to put a cap on the toothpaste anyway. We say this to her even though we would have demanded a refund if the movie had ended with Annie marrying Walter. If we actually believe the things we say to married Annie, then we shouldn't care how *Sleepless in Seattle* ends. In fact, if we truly believe that all of the Walters and Sams in the world can make all of the Annies equivalently happy and fulfilled, then we should find all romantic comedies and Jane Austen novels puzzling and pointless.

Of course, some people do find Jane Austen's stories puzzling and pointless. Other people believe that marriage vows should never be broken under any circumstance, which is a harsh but valid position. The Sacred Cow in this situation is not the belief that marriages should be preserved. Anyone who believes that divorce is immoral or that all human pairings are equally fulfilling should feel free to say so. However, anyone who has ever enjoyed a romance story understands that not every match is or can be equally wonderful. The romantics among us owe it to Annie (and to Walter) to either acknowledge their pain and tell them to suck it up, or get out of their way if they decide to divorce.

Conclusion

The Other Cow will always have a lot of fodder, because salacious stories are hard to resist. Sunshine will expose this Cow for what she really is, however. The Other Cow uses society's disapproval of adultery to keep people from leaving their marriages for new partners. She is dishonest about her motives, and she uses double standards to achieve her ends. The next time the Other Cow asks you to express shocked condemnation about a complicated divorce, ask yourself whether your condemnation is about infidelity or divorce. If somebody robbed a bank in order to afford a divorce lawyer, you would condemn the robbery, but you wouldn't say that the robber should have to stay married. Similarly, it's possible to agree with the Other Cow that adultery is bad without agreeing with her that nobody should get divorced.

References

1. Blow, A.J., Hartnett, K. (2005). Infidelity in committed relationships II: A substantive review. *Journal of Marital and Family Therapy*, 31, 217-233.

2. Wiederman, M.W. (1997). Extramarital sex: prevalence and correlates in a national survey. *Journal of Sex Research*, 34, 167-174.

3. Atkins, D.C., Baucom, D.H., Jacobson, N.S. (2001). Understanding infidelity: correlates in a national random sample. *Journal of Family Psychology*, 15, 735-749.

4. Forste, R., Tanfer, K. (1996). Sexual exclusivity among dating, cohabiting, and married women. *Journal of Marriage and the Family*, 58, 33–47.

5. Laumann, E.O., Gagnon, J.H., Michael, R.T., Michaels, S. (1994). *The social organization of sexuality*. Chicago IL: University of Chicago Press.

6. Glass, S.P., Staeheli, J.C. (2003). *Not "Just Friends": Rebuilding Trust and Recovering Your Sanity After Infidelity*. New York, NY: Free Press.

7. South, S.J., Lloyd, K.M. (1995). Spousal alternatives and marital dissolution. *American Sociological Review*, 60, 21–35.

8. Amato, P.R., Rogers, S.J. (1997). A Longitudinal Study of Marital Problems and Subsequent Divorce. *Journal of Marriage and Family*, 59 (3), 612-624.

Conclusion

Congratulations! You have successfully recognized and given some well-placed pushes to seven Sacred Cows of Marriage and Divorce to see how easily they tip. Now that you have met all seven Sacred Cows, let's test your Cow sense:

Testing Your Cow Sense

For each question below, circle the answer that you think best completes the sentence.

Question 1: People who get divorced are:
A) sexually repressed
B) bad people
C) incapable of intimacy
D) people who probably shouldn't be married to each other

Question 2: Sexual desire derives from:
A) admiration
B) Barry Manilow
C) intimacy
D) I don't know, but I know it when I feel it

Question 3: The job of a marriage counselor should be:
A) to save the marriage
B) to tell your spouse what a jerk he/she is
C) to improve communication
D) to help you and your spouse become happier people

Question 4: After a divorce:
   A) financial problems arise
   B) all children become criminals
   C) hard feelings are normal
   D) sometimes everyone ends up happier

Question 5: True Love:
   A) is a cruel myth created by Disney
   B) cannot survive contact with the toothpaste test
   C) is hard to find
   D) is what most people want

Question 6: Typically, extramarital affairs end in:
   A) divorce
   B) someone crushed under a train
   C) forgiveness
   D) it depends

Question 7: Morality in marriage requires you to:
   A) keep calm and carry on
   B) close your eyes and think of the Queen
   C) put your spouse's best interest before your own
   D) find a respectful solution to your marital problems

Scoring Your Cow Sense

Give yourself one point for each question to which you answered D (D is always sufficiently vague that it could be right).

Give yourself a half a point for answers A or C. These might all be correct under the right circumstances.

Give yourself zero points for each question to which you answered B. Those answers are just silly.

0 to 3 points: You skipped to the back to take this quiz, didn't you?

4 to 5 points: We are guessing that you are an Anglophile who reads a lot of Tolstoy.

6 points: Fair enough; some people have a thing for Barry Manilow.

7 points: You are officially Cow-proof!

You may have found this quiz irritating, because it did not serve up a simple, correct answer for any of the questions. Life is like that too. Sadly, you cannot pick up a self-help book to receive a simple, straightforward, correct answer to your questions. Marriage and divorce are complicated, and just like the quiz, there are not a lot of clear-cut right answers. There are some answers that don't make sense, however, and those are the ones we have tried to dig up. You may not have agreed with us on every point, but we hope that you have gained some new perspectives about our society's attitudes towards marriage and divorce.

Let's look back and see what we have learned. Have we learned the magic formula for a happy marriage? Well, no. We haven't found that formula yet, but we promise to tell you when we do. Have we helped anybody to decide whether to stay married or divorce? No, we didn't cover that either. As promised at the beginning of this book, we haven't dispensed any good advice, we haven't provided easy steps to anything (unless you count Sacred Cow tipping), and we haven't even had the decency to say that everything will be okay. We certainly hope that everything will be okay, but we will leave predictions about the future to the self-help professionals.

There is a range of very good reasons for not getting divorced, the most obvious of which is that marriages sometimes get better. Even for couples who are chronically unhappy, divorce may not be a good option for financial reasons or because of complex family structures. What we have tried to do is show that our culture is not only happy to trot out these good reasons for avoiding divorce, but in its eagerness to prevent disruption, our society also trots out some thinly disguised Sacred Cows. We have tried to identify these Cows, examine why and how our society uses them, and through scrutiny and logic, tip them over.

Our goal in exposing the Sacred Cows of Marriage and Divorce is most certainly not to encourage divorce. Our goal is

DANIELLE TELLER & ASTRO TELLER

to make it possible for each person facing the issue of divorce to do so without the added guilt and confusion created by a stampede of Sacred Cows.

We have tried to make this book fun to read and to show that humor is an excellent defense against Sacred Cows. But humor aside, there are many people caught agonizingly between the reality of how they feel and the Sacred Cows that forbid them from even exploring divorce as an option. It is our sincere hope that if this book does nothing else, it can give some people in this situation the permission to examine their situation openly and thoughtfully and without guilt or shame. If you know someone who is going through such a situation, please pass this message on to them: "The Sacred Cows that haunt you aren't of your making and they aren't your problem. Work through your marriage with compassion for yourself, your spouse, and your children. The Sacred Cows don't need or deserve your attention or your energy."

We wish for you and for all who you hold dear that love be central all the days of your life and theirs.

Acknowledgments

We would like to thank Lori Gottlieb, Philip Cohen and Esther Perel for being willing to share their expertise with us. As Socrates said, "True wisdom comes to each of us when we realize how little we understand about life, ourselves, and the world around us." These smart people made us much wiser about how little we know.

To Jacqueline Munro, Dave Andre, Liese Schwarz, Genevieve LeClaire, Jennifer Bird, Karen Mueller, Peter Stone, Zander Teller, Bob Dyck, Christopher Shreenan-Dyck, John Girard, and Rory Dyck: You rock. Thank you for helping to bring the Cows to life.

We must also thank Dana Boadway Masson for the wonderful cow illustrations. We wish that the rest of the book were as fabulous as her creations.

We owe a great debt of gratitude to our agents, Jim Levine and Kerry Sparks at Levine Greenberg Rostan. They were willing to take a chance on this unusual project, and they worked tirelessly to get the message about *Sacred Cows* to the people who might benefit from it. Their faith in the worth of this project has meant a great deal to us.

Finally, we must thank the diligent, talented, resourceful and (most important of all) forgiving team at Diversion Books. Mary Cummings and her colleagues Sarah Masterson Hally, Brielle Benton and Hannah Black have put up with our ignorance about publishing with the utmost grace and good humor, and they have turned our amateur scribbling into the respectable product that you now hold in your hand.

About the Authors

Astro Teller and Danielle Teller are qualified to write this book not by the M.D.s and Ph.D.s after their names—although they do happen to have M.D.s and Ph.D.s after their names. They are not famous professors of psychology, and they have not written hundreds of professional journal articles or received numerous prestigious awards for their extensive contributions to marriage and family research. Their areas of professional expertise have nothing to do with marriage and divorce. However, they have both been divorced, and they are happily married now. They are passionate about marriage as a concept, an institution and the most potentially joyful of all possible states a human being can achieve.

CPSIA information can be obtained
at www.ICGtesting.com
Printed in the USA
BVOW11s1303020518
515048BV00006B/676/P